DIGITAL TRADE FACILITATION IN ASIA AND THE PACIFIC

Edited by

Yann Duval
and
Alexey Kravchenko

STUDIES IN TRADE, INVESTMENT AND INNOVATION 87

DIGITAL TRADE FACILITATION IN ASIA AND THE PACIFIC

United Nations Publications
Sales No. E.18.II.F.10
Copyright © United Nations 2017
All rights reserved
Manufactured in Thailand
ISBN: 978-92-1-120774-3
eISBN: 978-92-1-363122-5
ST/ESCAP/2811
Print ISSN: 1020-3516
Online ISSN: 2414-0953

For further information on this publication, please contact:

Mia Mikic
Director
Trade, Investment and Innovation Division
United Nations Economic and Social Commission for Asia and the Pacific
United Nations Building
Rajadamnern Nok Avenue
Bangkok 10200, Thailand
E-mail: escap-tiid@un.org

Reference to dollars($) are to United States dollar unless otherwise stated.

Acknowledgements

This publication was prepared by Yann Duval, Chief, Trade Policy and Facilitation Section (TPFS), Trade, Investment and Innovation Division (TIID), ESCAP and Alexey Kravchenko, Associate Economic Affairs Officer, TPFS, under the overall supervision of Mia Mikic, Director, TIID, ESCAP. Chapter 1 was drafted jointly by Yann Duval, Tengfei Wang and Alexey Kravchenko, all from TIID. Chapter 2 was co-authored by Yann Duval, Chorthip Utoktham (consultant, TIID) and Alexey Kravchenko, while chapter 3 was drafted by Yann Duval and Kong Mengjing (Graduate legal research intern, TIID). Sung Heun Ha, Director, Korea Trade Network (KTNET), Tahseen Khan, Vice-Chair of the UN Centre for Trade Facilitation and Electronic Business (UN/CEFACT) and Advisory Committee Member of the United Nations Network of Experts for Paperless Trade and Transport in Asia and the Pacific (UNNExT) and Yann Duval co-authored chapter 4. Research assistance from Agathe Blanchard, Carlos Maria Mancini, Vyonna Bondi and Ying Liu is greatly appreciated.

The papers included in this publication benefited greatly from reviews, suggestions and inputs from Hong Xue (BNU, China), Luca Castellani (UNCITRAL), Biswajit Nag (IIFT), Sangwon Lim and Yuhua Zhang (ESCAP), Alisa Dicaprio (ADBI) and Akhmad Bayhaqi (APEC). Useful comments from participants to the Joint UN Regional Commissions side event on Trade Facilitation for Sustainable Development at the 4th OECD-WTO Aid for Trade Global Review (July 2017) and the ADBI-UNCTAD Workshop on Trade and the Digital Economy (November 2016), during which the content of chapters 1 and 3 were presented, are also gratefully acknowledged. Design and formatting of the publication for online dissemination was done by Erawan Printing with the support of Praiya Prayongsap and Pakkaporn Visetsilpanon (ESCAP). The financial support received from the Republic of Korea to conduct and disseminate this study is gratefully acknowledged.

Executive Summary

The simplification and digitalization of international trade procedures, or digital trade facilitation, is essential to reducing trade costs and enabling developing economies to effectively use trade as an engine of growth and sustainable development. Trade facilitation has taken increasing importance as evidenced by the entry into force of the World Trade Organization Trade Facilitation Agreement (WTO TFA). Governments in Asia and the Pacific have also engaged in a growing number of regional and subregional initiatives for facilitating the electronic exchange of information along international supply chains, including most recently the adoption of a Framework Agreement on Facilitation of Cross-border Paperless Trade in Asia and the Pacific (FA-PT), a United Nations treaty signed by Bangladesh, Cambodia, China, Armenia, and the Islamic Republic of Iran in 2017.[1]

In light of the increasing importance of digital trade facilitation, this report provides an overview of trade facilitation and paperless trade implementation in the Asia-Pacific region, followed by an analysis of the impact on trade costs of different sets of trade facilitation measures. It also reviews in some details paperless trade provisions in recent regional trade agreements in the region, before discussing the benefits of the FA-PT as an inclusive regional platform and tool to accelerate progress towards digital trade facilitation.

The first chapter presents key results of the second United Nations Global Survey on Trade Facilitation and Paperless Trade Implementation (UNTF Survey), covering 44 countries in Asia and the Pacific.[2] Despite existing efforts and initiatives, the results highlight the difficulties for the region in moving towards cross-border paperless trade: the average implementation rate of measures such as electronic exchange of Certificates of Origin, or of Sanitary and Phytosanitary Certificates stand at less than 20%, compared to more than 50% for most other types of trade facilitation measures. The findings also show that trade facilitation implementation rates vary widely across and within subregions. The analysis suggests that limited human resource capacity is a key challenge for Asia-Pacific least developed and landlocked developing countries in making further progress, while the lack of coordination between government agencies seems to be the most important challenge in other developing economies.

Chapter 2 estimates the effect of trade facilitation measures implementation on trade costs in Asia and the Pacific using data from the UNTF Survey. Impact of different sets of measures are considered, from a basic set of measures to ensure compliance with the WTO TFA commitments to a full set of digital trade facilitation measures. The analysis shows that full implementation of both binding and non-binding measures in the WTO TFA is associated with an average 15% trade cost reduction in Asia-Pacific. On the other hand, full implementation of binding and non-binding WTO TFA measures together with other paperless and cross-border trade facilitation measures (digital trade facilitation) is projected to decrease trade costs by more than 26%, cutting international transaction costs in Asia and the Pacific by about $1.2 trillion annually. The analysis also confirms that there are significant reductions in trade costs associated with trade partners' implementation of trade facilitation measures. This shows that economies which already have high rates of trade facilitation implementation have strong incentive to encourage and support their trading partners in implementing trade facilitation. Further facilitation of trade in these economies will involve developing legal and technical frameworks to support cross-border paperless trade, i.e., enabling the electronic exchange and legal recognition of trade data and documents between public and private actors located in different countries along the international supply chain, as envisaged in the recently adopted regional UN treaty on cross-border paperless trade facilitation (the FA-PT).

Next, chapter 3 analyses the extent to which recent regional trade agreements (RTAs) have included provisions related to paperless trade globally, using the WTO TFA as a reference. The results provide insights and models for future negotiations in this area, as well as for implementation of the FA-PT. The analysis revealed that more than half of the trade agreements which have entered into force since 2005 globally include paperless trade measures or provisions, with a large majority of RTAs now featuring one or more measures aiming to exchange trade-related data and information electronically. In many cases, recent RTAs are found to go further than the WTO TFA in promoting digital trade facilitation

---

[1]   As of December 2017.

[2]   Interactive database available at: https://unnext.unescap.org/AP_TFSurvey 2017.

and the application of modern information and communications technologies to trade procedures. Furthermore, many of the recent RTAs found in Asia and the Pacific implicitly or explicitly call upon the parties to develop electronic exchange of trade-related data and documents and work towards interoperability of paperless trade systems. However, they provide little detail on how to do so beyond recommending cooperation among the parties. In this context, the FA-PT provides a useful multilateral framework through which paperless trade-related RTA commitments may be concretized.

Finally, chapter 4 provides an overview of the FA-PT. The Framework Agreement is fully dedicated to the digitalization of trade processes and enabling the seamless electronic exchange and legal recognition of trade-related data and documents across borders, rather than only between stakeholders located in the same country. Developed by a diverse group of more than 25 Asia-Pacific economies at very different stages of development over four years, the Framework Agreement is designed as an inclusive and enabling platform that will benefit all participating economies regardless of where they stand in terms of trade facilitation implementation. Implementation of the Agreement is expected to greatly reduce transaction time and costs as well as increase regulatory compliance. Importantly, it will enable countries that have already initiated work at the bilateral or subregional levels to leverage that work and ensure that emerging regional and multilateral solutions more fully take into account such work.

Achieving cross-border paperless trade across the region is expected to be a long and difficult process, and it cannot be achieved without close collaboration between countries. The FA-PT is expected to support that process by providing a dedicated institutional framework for countries with proven political will to develop legal and technical solutions for cross-border paperless trade, including through pilot projects, capacity building and technical assistance. The Framework Agreement provides a unique tool for countries to better implement the WTO TFA, taking full advantage of emerging digital solutions and technologies. It is also expected to help countries meet commitments they have already made on paperless trade through RTAs and other agreements.

Going forward, digitalization offers immense potential to enhance trade facilitation implementation and further reduce trade costs in Asia and the Pacific. The *Framework Agreement on Facilitation of Cross-Border Paperless Trade in Asia and the Pacific* provides a unique opportunity for participating countries to accelerate electronic exchange of trade-related data and documents across borders and to overcome challenges on cross-border paperless trade.

Contents

Contents *(continued)*

List of Boxes

List of Tables

Contents *(continued)*

List of Figures

Contents *(continued)*

Abbreviations

ADB	Asian Development Bank
AEO	authorized economic operator
APEC	Asia-Pacific Economic Cooperation
APTIR	Asia-Pacific Trade and Investment Report
ASEAN	Association of Southeast Asian Nations
ASW	ASEAN Single Window Agreement
ATIGA	ASEAN Trade in Goods Agreement
BtoG	business to government
CA	Certification Authority
CII	World Bank Doing Business Credit Information Index
COO	certificate of origin
ECA	United Nations Economic Commission for Africa
ECE	United Nations Economic Commission for Europe
ECLAC	United Nations Economic Commission for Latin America and the Caribbean
ENEA	East and North-East Asia
ESCAP	United Nations Economic and Social Commission for Asia and the Pacific
ESCWA	United Nations Economic and Social Commission for Western Asia
ESW	electronic single window
EU	European Union
FA-PT	Framework Agreement on Facilitation of Cross-border Paperless Trade in Asia and the Pacific
GATT	General Agreement on Tariffs and Trade
GtoG	government to government
CSN	Country with Special Needs
GDP	Gross Domestic Product
ICT	information and communications technology
ITC	International Trade Centre
LSCI	Liner Shipping Connectivity Index
NCA	North and Central Asia
NTB	non-tariff barrier
NTFC	National Trade Facilitation Committee
OCO	Oceania Customs Organization
OECD	Organization for Economic Co-operation and Development
PIDE	Pacific island developing economy
RTA	regional trade agreement
RTA-IS	Regional Trade Agreements Information System (WTO)
SAARC	South Asian Association for Regional Cooperation

SDGs	Sustainable Development Goals
SEA	South-East Asia
SMEs	small and medium-sized enterprises or small and medium enterprises
SPS	sanitary and phytosanitary
SSWA	South and South-West Asia
TBT	technical barriers to trade
TF	trade facilitation
TFA	Trade Facilitation Agreement
TFAF	Trade Facilitation Agreement Facility
TFPI	trade facilitation and paperless trade implementation
TPP	Trans-Pacific Partnership Agreement
UN/CEFACT	United Nations Centre for Trade Facilitation and Electronic Business
UNCITRAL	United Nations Commission on International Trade Law
UNCTAD	United Nations Conference on Trade and Development
UNNExT	United Nations Network of Experts for Paperless Trade and Transport for Asia and the Pacific
UNRC	United Nations Regional Commission
UNTF Survey	United Nations Global Survey on Trade Facilitation and Paperless Trade Implementation 2017
WCO	World Customs Organization
WTO	World Trade Organization

Chapter 1

Towards digital trade facilitation implementation in Asia and the Pacific: State of play

1.1. Introduction

It is well understood that reducing trade costs is essential in enabling economies to effectively participate in regional and global value chains and continue to use trade as a main engine of growth and sustainable development. Reducing trade costs is possible through, for example, elimination of tariff and non-tariff barriers and enhancing physical connectivity. Another important venue to reduce trade costs is through trade facilitation. A recent ESCAP (2017) study found that moderate region-wide improvements in trade facilitation in Asia-Pacific could lift GDP by 0.32% annually between 2015 and 2030, which is equivalent to nearly $87 billion per year – 14 times more than under the tariff liberalization scenario considered in the same study. This result provides strong support for the policy framework on channelling trade and investment into sustainable development proposed in that study, in which trade facilitation is one of the four key components. More generally, it confirms that trade facilitation in general, and digital trade facilitation in particular, should be a top priority for policymakers.

Digital trade facilitation refers here to the application of modern information and communications technologies (ICTs) to procedures involved in moving physical goods across borders. It includes in particular measures enabling the exchange of electronic (rather than paper-based) data and documents among public and private stakeholders involved in an international trade transaction, i.e. cross-border paperless trade. Asia-Pacific economies have long strived to make trade procedures as efficient as possible, including through implementation of automated customs systems, electronic single windows and other digital customs and trade facilitation initiatives. These paperless trade measures are rapidly becoming essential not only to maintain trade competitiveness, but also to address the trade control and logistics challenges associated with an increase in small shipments and cross-border e-commerce.

Paperless trade is formally defined as trade "taking place on the basis of electronic communications, including exchange of trade-related data and documents in electronic form" in the Framework Agreement on Facilitation of Cross-border Paperless Trade in Asia and the Pacific (FA-PT), a new United Nations treaty adopted by Member States of ESCAP in May 2016. While the ultimate goal of paperless trade is to dematerialize and digitalize all information flows associated with a given transaction for all stakeholders, paperless trade initiatives generally focus on facilitating data and documents flows between businesses and government (BtoG) and/or between governments (GtoG). Paperless trade generates significant economy-wide savings, including direct savings to traders in the form of lower compliance costs, as well as indirect savings from faster movement of goods, lower inventory costs and optimal use of transport and logistics infrastructure. It also enhances opportunities for small and medium enterprises (SMEs) to participate in cross-border trade, affords timely availability of shipping documents and reduces errors associated with re-keying of data.

Furthermore, the use of electronic rather than paper documents can also help enhance regulatory control and compliance by governments, especially when relevant data and documents can be exchanged among agencies and across borders. Indeed, the availability or more accurate and timely data in electronic form can enable trade control agencies to more efficiently evaluate the compliance risks associated with individual shipments, enabling them to identify high-risk transactions, ultimately boosting customs revenue while also speeding up the trade of compliant traders.

In that context, this study provides an overview of the state of trade facilitation in the Asia-Pacific region, with a specific focus on digital trade facilitation. This chapter briefly reviews trade costs in Asia and the Pacific, provides an update on the WTO Trade Facilitation Agreement (TFA), and discusses the results of the UN Global Survey on Trade Facilitation and Paperless Trade Implementation 2017. Chapter 2 features an analysis of the impact on trade costs of different sets of trade facilitation measures, from minimum WTO TFA compliance to full digital trade facilitation. Chapter 3 in turn analyses paperless trade provisions in recent regional trade agreements. Chapter 4 provides an overview of the Framework Agreement on Facilitation of Cross-border Paperless Trade in Asia and the Pacific, as a tool to accelerate progress towards digital trade facilitation.

1.2. Trade costs in Asia and the Pacific

Reducing trade costs is essential in enabling economies to effectively participate in global value chains and use trade as a main engine of growth and sustainable development. Following Arvis et al. (2013), trade costs are comprehensively defined here as the difference between all costs involved in trading goods bilaterally and those involved in trading goods domestically. As such, they include international shipping and logistic costs, policy barriers (tariff and non-tariff costs), legal and regulatory costs, and costs associated with the use of different languages and currencies.

Figure 1.1 shows the evolution of trade costs of the Asia-Pacific subregions in trading with the three largest developed economies from 1996 to 2014.[1] The trade cost levels in the Asia-Pacific region have typically remained similar across time, and still vary widely across subregions. East Asia-3 has the lowest trade costs of the region, only slightly higher than those of the European Union EU-3. North and Central Asian economies have seen sharper trade cost reductions than other subregions over the past decade, and now face trade costs comparable to the ones of South Asian economies (SAARC-4). Trade costs remain the highest in the Pacific island developing economies, and a clear trend towards lower trade costs is not apparent in that subregion.

Figure 1.1. Trade costs of Asia-Pacific subregions with large developed economies, 1996-2014

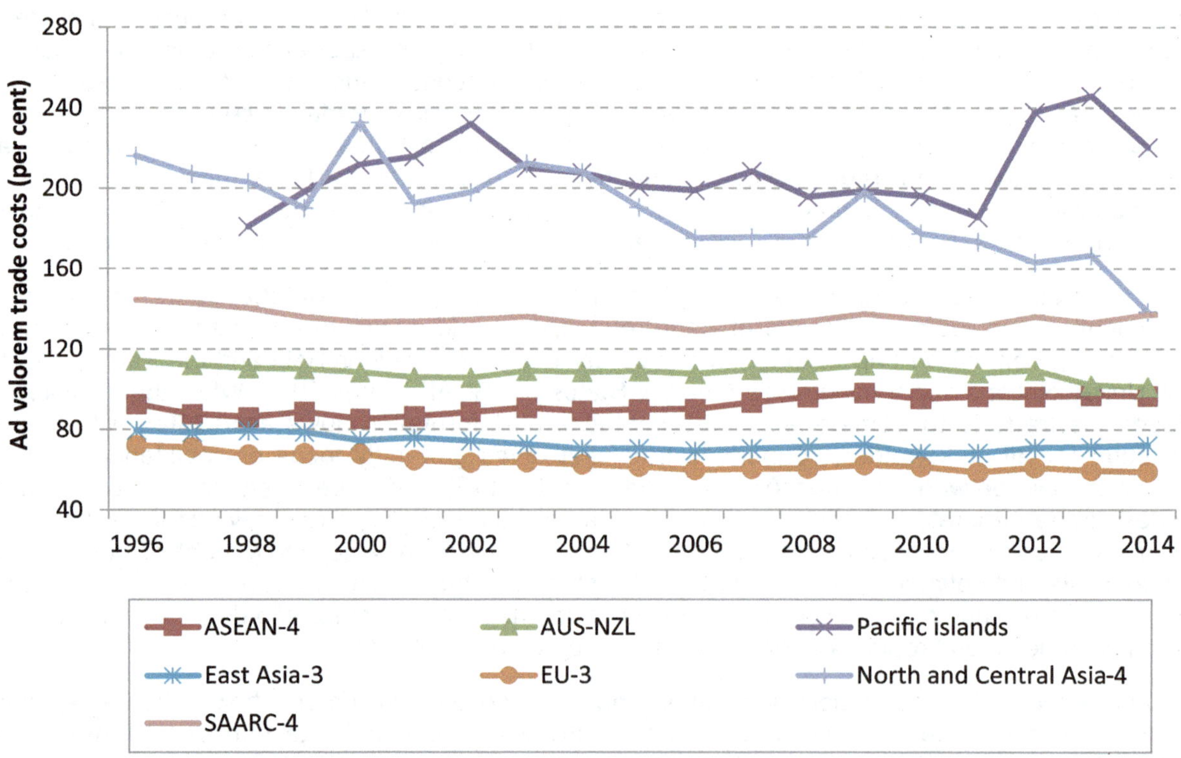

Source: ESCAP-World Bank Trade Costs Database (accessed June 2017).

Note: ASEAN-4 – Indonesia, Malaysia, the Philippines and Thailand; AUS-NZL – Australia and New Zealand; East Asia-3 – China, Japan and the Republic of Korea; EU-3 – Germany, France and the United Kingdom; Pacific Islands-2 – Fiji and Papua New Guinea; North and Central Asia-4 – Georgia, Kazakhstan, Kyrgyzstan and the Russian Federation; and SAARC-4 – Bangladesh, India, Pakistan and Sri Lanka. Trade costs shown are tariff equivalents, calculated as trade-weighted average trade costs of countries in each subregion with the three largest developed economies (Germany, Japan and the United States).

---

[1] This is done using bilateral aggregate trade cost data from the ESCAP-World Bank Trade Cost Database, available at: https://artnet.unescap.org/database.

Intra and extra-regional trade costs of the various Asia-Pacific subregions are shown in table 1.1. The subregional groupings that exhibit the lowest intraregional trade costs are East Asia-3 and AUS-NZL (51%) for 2010-2015. Both regions have seen their intraregional trade costs fall during 2010-2015 when compared to the 2009-2014 average (2.9% decrease for East-Asia-3, 4.9% decrease for AUS-NZL). In contrast, the Pacific islands have the highest intraregional trade cost (130%), more than twice the intraregional trade costs of the regional benchmark, East Asia-3, even if it still slowly decreases (-8.8% during 2010-2015 when compared to 2009-2014).

As expected, intraregional trade costs are generally significantly lower than extraregional trade costs. There are exceptions, however. Intraregional trade costs of ASEAN are similar to those between ASEAN and East Asia-3. Intra-SAARC trade costs are slightly higher than trade costs between South Asian economies and the United States or the EU. Finally, extraregional trade costs between Pacific islands and AUS-NZL are much lower (82%) than trade costs among the Pacific islands themselves.

Table 1.1. Intra- and extraregional comprehensive non-tariff trade costs in the Asia-Pacific region

Region	ASEAN-4	East Asia-3	North and Central Asia-4	Pacific Islands Developing Economies	SAARC-4	AUS-NZL	EU-3
ASEAN-4	76% (6.7%)						
East Asia-3	76% (4.1%)	51% (-2.9%)					
North and Central Asia-4	343% (5.4%)	167% (-9.9%)	116% (-0.9%)				
Pacific Islands Developing Economies	172% (-9.0%)	173% (-3.1%)	370% (21.6%)	130% (-8.8%)			
SAARC-4	130% (3.5%)	123% (-2.1%)	302% (7.7%)	300% (-4.6%)	119% (12.9%)		
AUS-NZL	101% (2.9%)	87% (-5.4%)	341% (-4.9%)	82% (-8.9%)	136% (-6.7%)	51% (-4.9%)	
EU-3	105% (-3.4%)	84% (-3.4%)	150% (-7.1%)	204% (-7.1%)	113% (0.3%)	108% (-2.3%)	42% (-8.1%)
United States	86% (8.0%)	63% (0.4%)	174% (-3.5%)	161% (-5.4%)	112% (6.7%)	100% (2.9%)	67% (0.4%)

Source: ESCAP-World Bank Trade Costs Database (accessed June 2017).
Note: Trade costs shown are average trade costs during 2010-2015 and may be interpreted as tariff equivalents. Changes in average trade costs between 2004-2009 and 2010-2015 are in parenthesis. Refer to the note in figure 4.1 for details of country groupings.

Figure 1.2 shows trade costs evolution between countries with special needs and the three largest developed economies. Trade costs of countries with special needs are found to be two to three times higher than those experienced by East Asia-3 (the regional benchmark). The small island developing States experience the highest trade costs. Of greatest concern is the fact that trade costs for this set of countries appear to have increased over time (from 302% to 319% between 2013 and 2014). This is essentially explained by rising trade costs for the small islands developing states, as Asia-Pacific least developed countries have experienced declining trade costs since 2009, while trade costs of landlocked developing countries in the region have also fallen slightly over the past decade. From 267% in 2009, least developed countries trade costs dropped to 193% in 2014.

Overall, trade costs in the Asia-Pacific region remain heterogeneous. There is no strong trend towards convergence in trade costs between subregions that experience higher intra- and extraregional trade costs and those for which trade costs are relatively lower. Furthering regional integration agendas and ensuring that international trade continues to be an engine for growth will require addressing the disparities in trade costs. Over the past decade, most of the trade cost reductions have been achieved through the elimination or lowering of tariffs, implying that further trade costs reduction now has to come from other sources. As a matter of fact, a recent study conducted by the ESCAP and other UNRCs[2] showed that a 10% increase in the implementation of trade facilitation measures could result in a 2.8% decrease in trade costs.

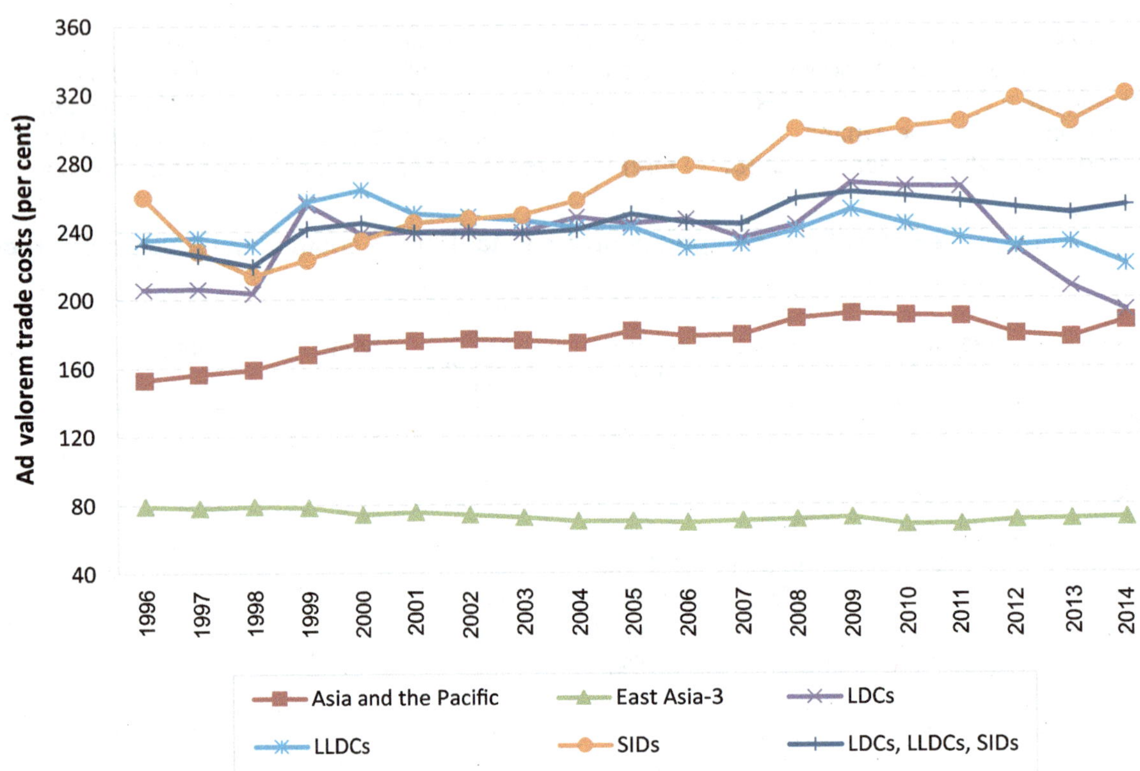

Figure 1.2. Trade costs of Asia-Pacific countries with special needs and large developed economies, 1996-2014

Sources: ESCAP-World Bank Trade Cost Database (accessed June 2017).
Note: The trade costs shown are tariff equivalents, calculated as trade-weighted average trade costs of countries in each group with the three largest developed economies (Germany, Japan and the United States). LDCs: Least developed countries; LLDCs: Landlocked developing countries; SIDS: Small island developing states.

1.3. WTO Trade Facilitation Agreement: An update

The World Trade Organization Trade Facilitation Agreement (WTO TFA), concluded in 2013 at the Bali Ministerial Conference, entered into force on 22 February 2017 following its ratification by two-third of the WTO member States. As of 8 December 2017, 125 out of the 164 WTO members have ratified the treaty, 32 of them are ESCAP regional member States and associate members. The objective of the WTO TFA is to facilitate the movement, clearance and release of goods through more efficient customs and border procedures. It also aims to foster effective cooperation between customs on trade facilitation issues.[3]

In order to reach these goals, a Trade Facilitation Agreement Facility (TFAF) was created to help developing and least-developed countries obtaining the assistance they need. Technical assistance (provided by the WTO, the World Bank, the World Customs Organization, and the United Nations Conference on Trade and Development) and capacity building are key elements in the implementation of the Agreement which might, based on the WTO estimates, reduce trade costs by 14.3% and boost global trade by $1 trillion per year.

---

[2] ESCAP (2015)

[3] The WTO TFA comprises 12 sections : (i) publication and availability of information, (ii) opportunity to comment, information before entry into force, and consultations, (iii) advance rulings, (iv) procedures for appeal or review, (v) other measures to enhance impartiality, non-discrimination and transparency, (vi) disciplines on fees and charges imposed on or in connection with importation and exportation and penalties, (vii) release and clearance of goods, (viii) border agency cooperation, (ix) movement of goods intended for import under customs control, (x) formalities connected with importation, exportation and transit, (xi) freedom of transit, (xii) customs cooperation.

Out of the 32 ESCAP member States of the Asia-Pacific region that have ratified the TFA, 25 have already submitted notifications of relevant provisions of the TFA. In addition, a further four ESCAP members States have submitted notifications in anticipation of the TFA ratification. Members must notify when they will implement each trade facilitation measure using three different categories: category A notifications indicate the provisions that the WTO members have implemented by the time the Agreement entered into force (or in the case of a least-developed country within one year after entry into force); category B notifications indicate provisions that the member will implement after a transitional period following the entry into force of the Agreement; and category C contains provisions that the member will implement on a date after a transitional period following the entry into force of the Agreement and requiring the acquisition of assistance and support for capacity building.

Figure 1.3. Notifications of the WTO TFA by Asia-Pacific economies (percentage of articles)

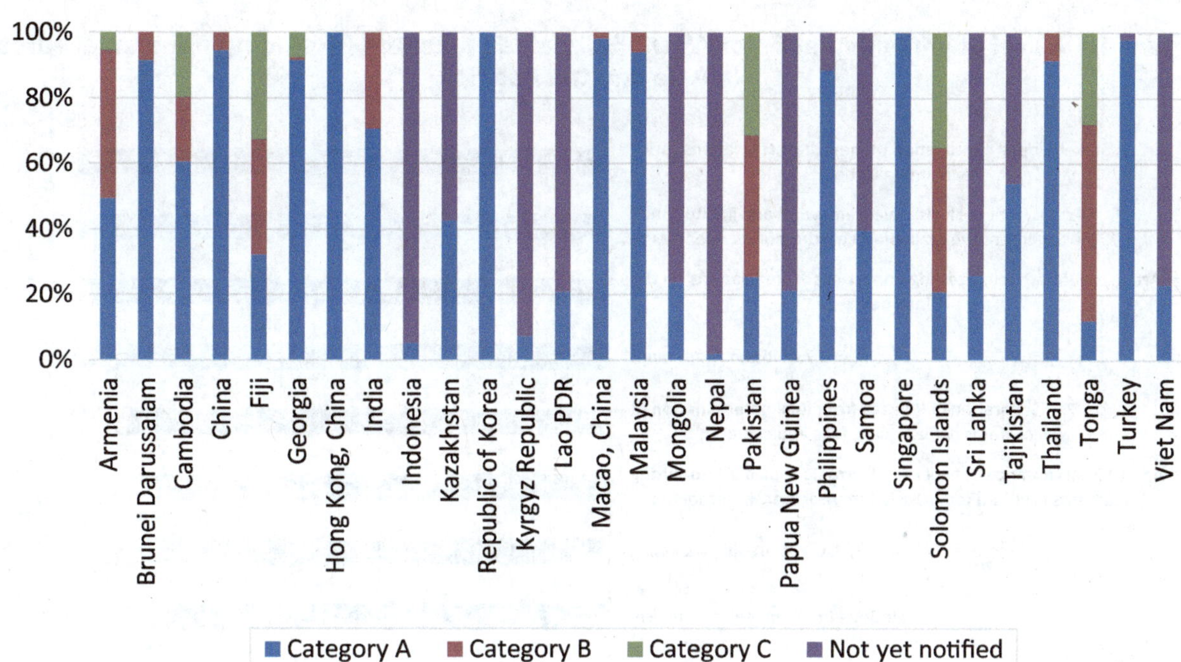

Source:　WTO Trade Facilitation Agreement database (accessed December 2017).

Figure 1.3 shows the level of notification by country, providing some indication of the level of trade facilitation implementation and policy priorities among the members. There are strong disparities between economies. Three members have fully notified all Articles of the TFA under category A (the Republic of Korea, Singapore, and Hong Kong, China) and another eight economies have notified more than 90% of the Agreement under Category A. In contrast, six economies have only notified around 20% of the Articles (Indonesia, Kyrgyzstan, Nepal, Viet Nam, Papua New Guinea and the Lao People's Democratic Republic).

The most notified trade facilitation measures under category A in Asia-Pacific countries are: use of customs brokers, common border procedures, specific disciplines on fees and charges, and penalty disciplines. These measures are all related to Article 6 (disciplines on fees and charges imposed on or in connection with importation and exportation and penalties) or Article 10 (formalities connected with importation, exportation and transit). However, it seems that implementation of Article 7 (release and clearance of goods) in the region may be more problematic, as the three least notified measures (risk management, average release times, authorized operators) all belong to this article. It is worth noting, however, that Category A notifications may not fully reflect the implementation situation and are likely to underestimate it, as in the case of Indonesia (see box 1.1 and section 1.4 in this chapter).

Box 1.1. WTO TFA Articles implementation in Asia and the Pacific

The United Nations Regional Commissions recently released the results of the UN Global Survey on Trade Facilitation and Paperless Trade Implementation 2017, which features many of the provisions included in the WTO TFA. Figure 1.4 shows the level of implementation of the WTO TFA Articles in Asia and the Pacific based on this new dataset. The most "at least partially implemented" measures in the Asia-Pacific region are Article 2, *Stakeholders' consultation on new draft regulations* (prior to their finalization), Article 8, *National legislative framework and institutional arrangement are available to ensure border agencies cooperate with each other*, and Article 1.2 *Publication of existing import-export regulations on the internet*. These measures have been at least partially implemented by over 90% of ESCAP member States. The least implemented measure is Article 10.4 *Electronic Single Window System*, with full and partial implementation implemented by fewer than 40% of ESCAP member States, though some economies have entered the pilot stage of implementation.

Figure 1.4. Level of implementation of WTO TFA related measures (excluding transit measures) in Asia and the Pacific

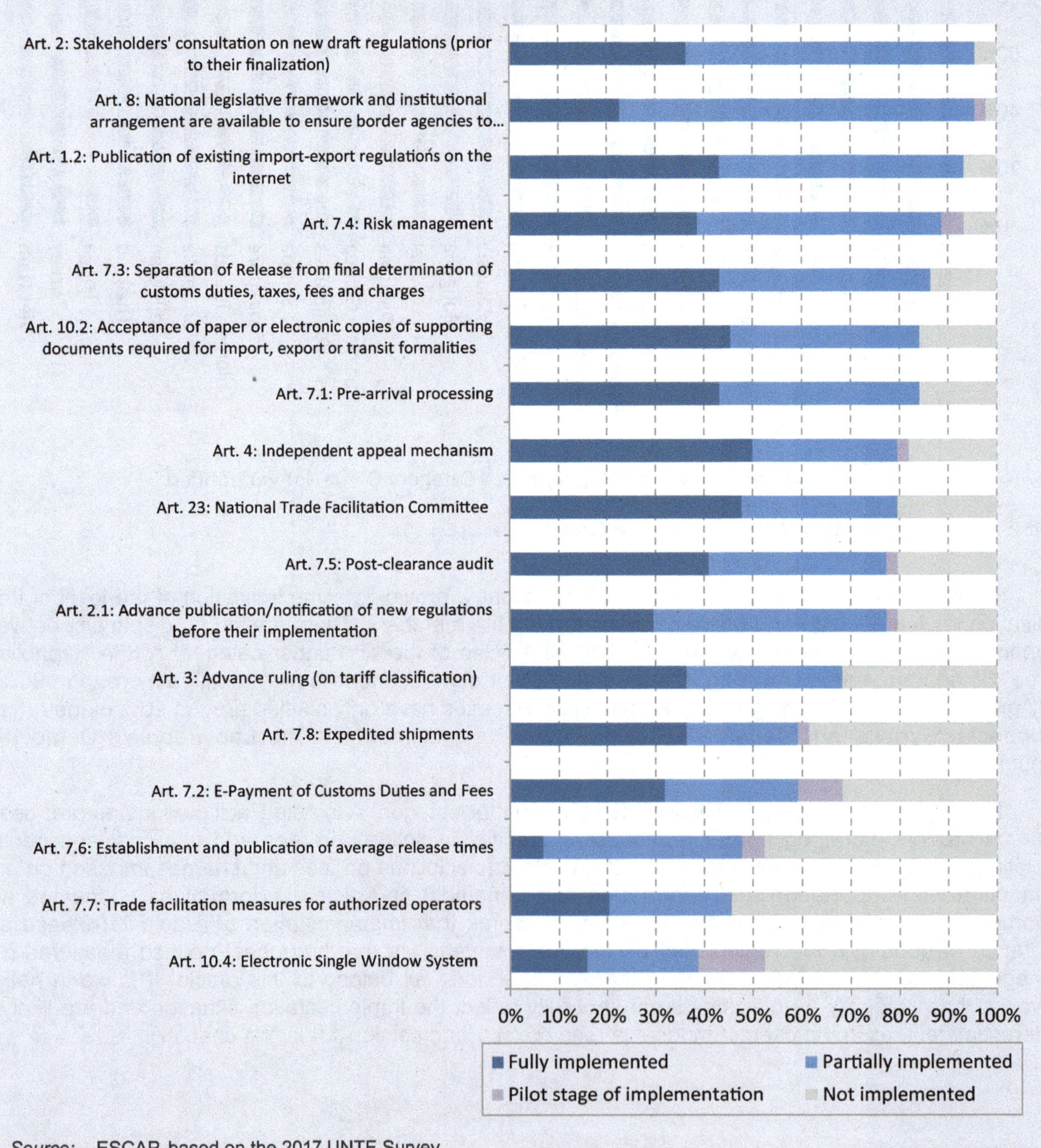

Source: ESCAP, based on the 2017 UNTF Survey.

1.4. Trade facilitation implementation in Asia-Pacific

The data presented in this section is based on the results of the second United Nations (UN) Global Survey on Trade Facilitation and Paperless Trade Implementation, which was conducted during the first half of 2017 and included 44 Asia-Pacific economies. The survey instrument was prepared according to the final list of commitments included in the World Trade Organization (WTO) Trade Facilitation Agreement (TFA), as well as to measures relevant to the ESCAP Framework Agreement on Facilitation of Cross-border Paperless Trade in Asia and the Pacific[4] and the 2030 Agenda for Sustainable Development. As such, the survey covers 47 main trade facilitation measures which are categorized into seven groups, namely: 1) General trade facilitation measures, 2) Paperless trade, 3) Cross-border paperless trade, 4) Transit facilitation, 5) Trade facilitation and SMEs, 6) Trade facilitation and agricultural trade and 7) Women and trade facilitation.

The General trade facilitation measures and Transit facilitation measures are largely covered by the WTO TFA. In contrast, very few paperless trade measures are specifically included in the WTO TFA. To capture the inclusive aspects of trade facilitation in the context of the Sustainable Development Goals (SDGs), three further groups of trade facilitation (TF) measures including "trade facilitation for SMEs", "trade facilitation for agricultural trade" and "women and trade facilitation" were added to the survey in 2017 (see table 1.2). These groups were not included in the previous surveys. Survey methodology is discussed in detail in ESCAP (2017b).[5]

Table 1.2. Grouping of trade facilitation measures included in the questionnaire

	Grouping	Trade facilitation measure (and question No.) in the questionnaire
General TF measures	Transparency	2. Publication of existing import-export regulations on the Internet 3. Stakeholder consultation on new draft regulations (prior to their finalization) 4. Advance publication/notification of new regulation before their implementation (e.g., 30 days prior) 5. Advance ruling (on tariff classification) 9. Independent appeal mechanism (for traders to appeal customs and other relevant trade control agencies' rulings)
	Formalities	6. Risk management (as a basis for deciding whether a shipment will be or not physically inspected) 7. Pre-arrival processing 8. Post-clearance audit 10. Separation of release from final determination of customs duties, taxes, fees and charges 11. Establishment and publication of average release times 12. Trade facilitation measures for authorized operators 13. Expedited shipments 14. Acceptance of paper or electronic copies of supporting documents required for import, export or transit formalities
	Institutional arrangement and cooperation	1. Establishment of a national trade facilitation committee or similar body 31. Cooperation between agencies on the ground at the national level 32. Government agencies delegating controls to Customs Authorities 33. Alignment of working days and hours with neighbouring countries at border crossings 34. Alignment of formalities and procedures with neighbouring countries at border crossings

---

[4] Available from http://www.unescap.org/resources/framework-agreement-facilitation-cross-border-paperless-trade-asia-and-pacific

[5] An interactive database of survey results as well as subregional and country reports are available from https://unnext.unescap.org/content/un-global-survey-trade-facilitation-and-paperless-trade-implementation-2017

Table 1.2. *(continued)*

Grouping	Trade facilitation measure (and question No.) in the questionnaire
Paperless trade	15. Electronic/automated Customs System established (e.g., ASYCUDA)
	16. Internet connection available to Customs and other trade control agencies at border-crossings
	17. Electronic Single Window System
	18. Electronic submission of customs declarations
	19. Electronic application and issuance of Trade Licenses
	20. Electronic submission of Sea Cargo Manifests
	21. Electronic submission of Air Cargo Manifests
	22. Electronic application and issuance of Preferential Certificate of Origin
	23. E-Payment of customs duties and fees
	24. Electronic application for customs refunds
Cross-border paperless trade	25. Laws and regulations for electronic transactions are in place (e.g. e-commerce law, e-transaction law)
	26. Recognized certification authority issuing digital certificates to traders to conduct electronic transactions
	27. Engagement of the country in trade-related cross-border electronic data exchange with other countries
	28. Certificate of Origin electronically exchanged between your country and other countries
	29. Sanitary & Phyto-Sanitary Certificate electronically exchanged between your country and other countries
	30. Banks and insurers in your country retrieving letters of credit electronically without lodging paper-based documents
Transit facilitation	35. Transit facilitation agreement(s) with neighbouring country(ies)
	36. Customs Authorities limit the physical inspections of transit goods and use risk assessment
	37. Supporting pre-arrival processing for transit facilitation
	38. Cooperation between agencies of countries involved in transit
Trade facilitation and SMEs	39. Government has developed trade facilitation measures that ensure easy and affordable access for SMEs to trade related information
	40. Government has developed specific measures that enable SMEs to more easily benefit from the AEO scheme
	41. Government has taken actions to make the single windows more easily accessible to SMEs (e.g., by providing technical consultation and training services to SMEs on registering and using the facility.)
	42. Government has taken actions to ensure that SMEs are well represented and made key members of National Trade Facilitation Committees (NTFCs)
Trade facilitation and agricultural trade	43. Testing and laboratory facilities are equipped for compliance with sanitary and phytosanitary (SPS) standards in your country
	44. National standards and accreditation bodies are established for the purpose of compliance with SPS standards in your country
	45. Application, verification and issuance of SPS certificates is automated
Women and trade facilitation	46. The existing trade facilitation policy/strategy incorporates special consideration of women involved in trade
	47. Government has introduced trade facilitation measures to benefit women involved in trade

Source: UN Global Survey on Trade Facilitation and paperless Trade Implementation, 2017

1.4.1. An overview of implementation in Asia-Pacific

Figure 1.5 shows the overall implementation levels of 44 Asia-Pacific economies based on a common set of 31 trade facilitation and paperless trade measures included in the survey.[6] The regional average implementation of this comprehensive set of trade facilitation measures stands at 50.4%. The implementation of trade facilitation measures in the region is very heterogeneous. Australia, Republic of Korea, Singapore, China and Japan achieve implementation rates in excess of 80%, while implementation among several Pacific island developing economies barely reaches 15%.

Figure 1.5. Overall implementation of trade facilitation measures in 44 Asia-Pacific countries, 2017

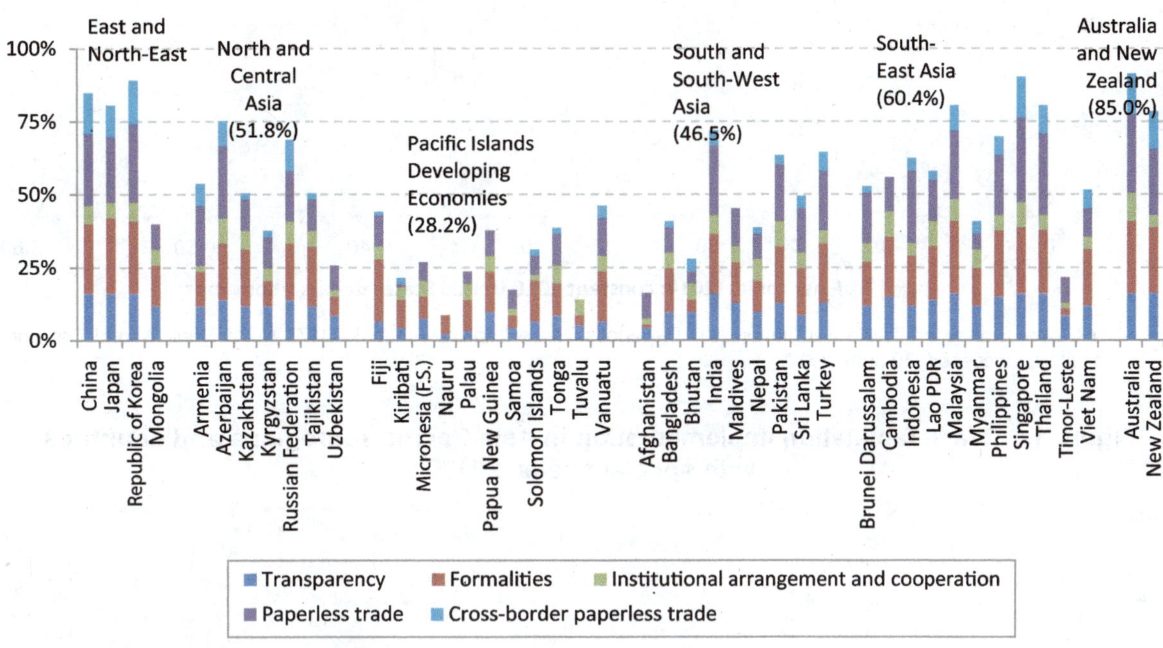

Source: UN Global Survey on Trade Facilitation and Paperless Trade Implementation, 2017

In general, higher economic development is associated with a higher level of implementation (figure 1.6). However, this is not always the case. For example, while Cambodia and the Lao People's Democratic Republic are classified as least developed countries, both achieve high implementation rates. Similarly, the Maldives achieves a relatively high score although it is a small island developing state that only recently graduated from the least developed country group.

1.4.2. Implementation in subregions and countries with special needs

Figure 1.7 presents an overview of the implementation of trade facilitation measures in the subregions and the groups of countries with special needs, namely, landlocked developing countries, Least developed countries and small islands developing states.[7] Aside from Australia and New Zealand (AU&NZ), East and North-East Asia (ENEA) achieved the highest average level of implementation at 74%, followed by South-East Asia (SEA), North and Central Asia (NCA) and South and South-West Asia (SSWA). Pacific island developing economies (PIDEs) lag far behind other subregions at 28%.

---

[6] Among the 47 trade facilitation measures surveyed, three measures including Electronic Submission of Sea Cargo Manifests (No. 20), Alignment of working days and hours with neighbouring countries at border crossings (No. 33), and Alignment of formalities and procedures with neighbouring countries at border crossings (No. 34) were excluded in calculating the overall score as they are not applicable to all countries surveyed. Similarly, four transit facilitation measures were also excluded. Three groups of trade facilitation measures related to SMEs, agricultural and women (measures 39-47) were excluded due to unavailability of data for some countries.

[7] See Annex A1 for country groups definitions.

**Figure 1.6. Trade facilitation implementation and GDP per capita
of 44 Asia-Pacific economies**

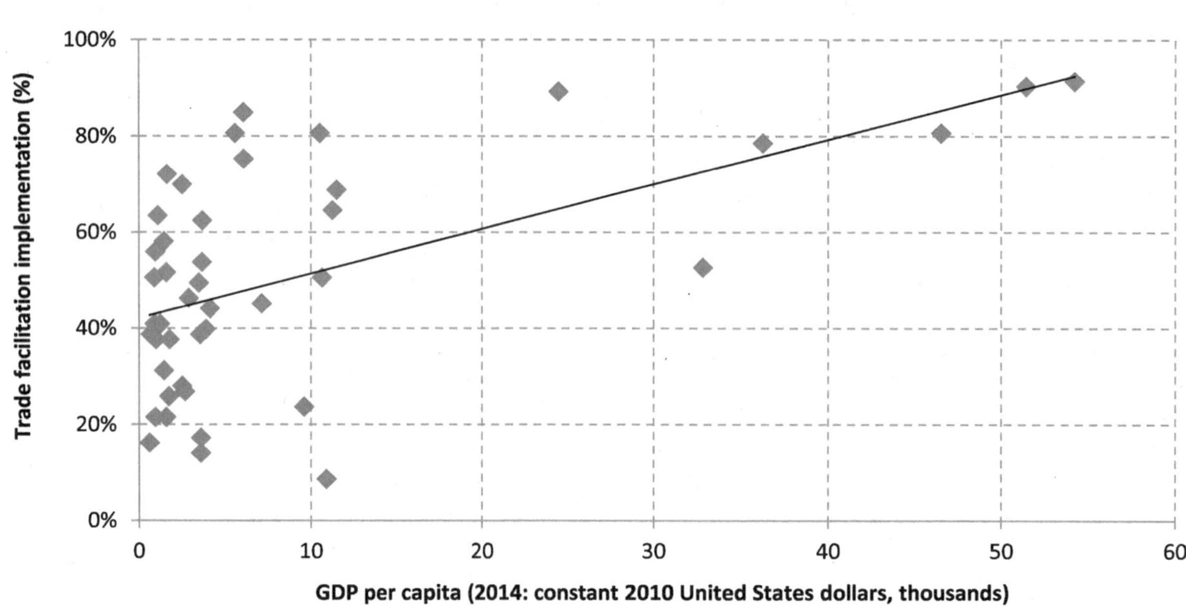

Sources: UN Global Survey on Trade Facilitation and Paperless Trade Implementation, 2017; World Bank, World Development Indicators, accessed 30 June 2017.

**Figure 1.7. Trade facilitation implementation in Asia-Pacific subregions and countries
with special needs, 2017[8]**

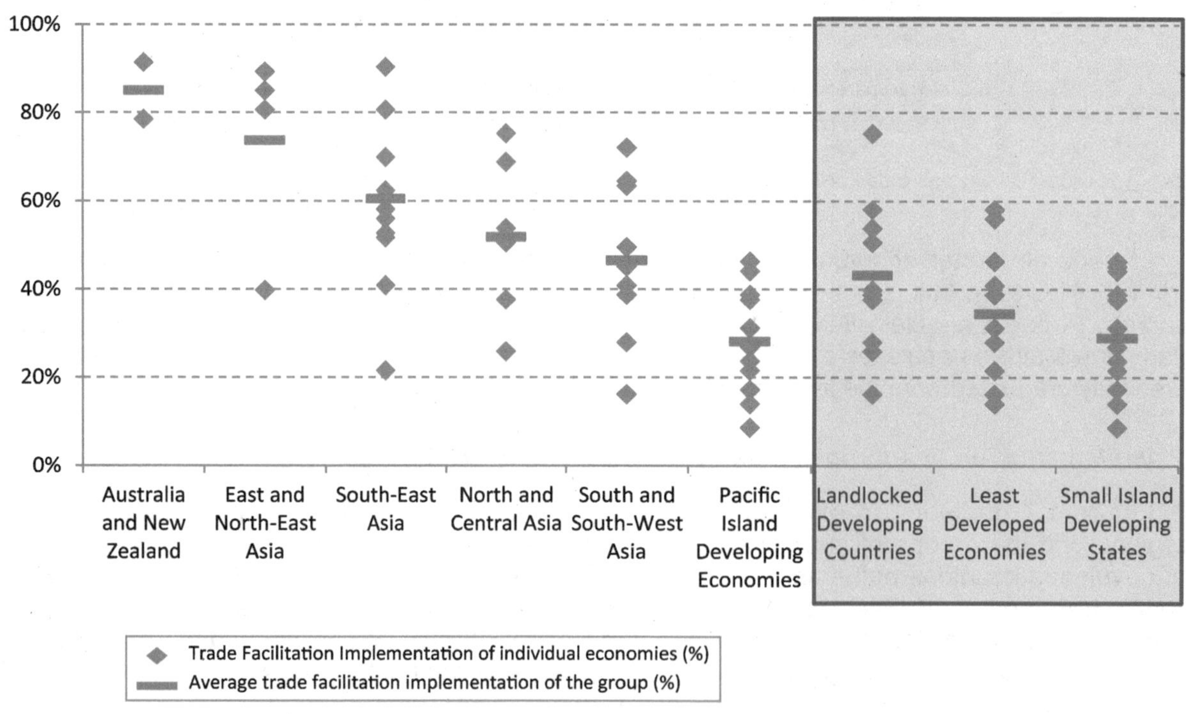

Source: UN Global Survey on Trade Facilitation and Paperless Trade Implementation, 2017

Trade facilitation implementation varies widely within each subregional grouping. Differences in trade facilitation implementation levels are widest in the South-East Asia subregion. Despite this, regional integration processes appear to have played a significant and positive role in trade facilitation implementation, and the South-East Asia subregion has achieved higher average implementation rate than several other subregions (such as North and Central Asia, South and South-West Asia and Pacific

---

[8]   Ibid

island developing economies). Differences in trade facilitation implementation levels are smallest within Pacific island developing economies. This may be explained by the fact that these small and generally isolated economies face similar implementation constraints.

Countries with special needs in the Asia-Pacific region face certain challenges in implementation of trade facilitation, in particular paperless trade and cross-border paperless trade measures (see figure 1.7). Landlocked developing countries as a group appear to have achieved higher levels of trade facilitation on average than least developed countries or small islands developing statess. This should be viewed as an important achievement in the context of the Vienna Programme of Action (VPoA), which aims to contribute to the eradication of poverty stemming from their landlockedness.[9]

1.4.3. Most and least implemented trade facilitation measures

All countries are engaged in implementation of various "transparency" and "formalities" measures. As shown in figure and table 1.3, "transparency" measures such as *Stakeholder consultation on new draft regulations prior to implementation* have been the most implemented: regional average implementation rate amounts to 68.5%. Implementation rate of "Formalities" measures reaches 60%. Regional average implementation of the "institutional arrangements and inter-agency cooperation" and "transit" measures is over 50%.

The regional average level of implementation of "paperless trade" measures also stands close to 50%. While many economies have developed legal frameworks to enable paperless trade, implementation of "cross-border paperless trade" has yet to begin in many developing countries and the average rate of implementation stands at 23%.

Figure 1.8 shows that agricultural trade facilitation has been generally well implemented. However, very few countries have customized trade facilitation measures to support small and medium enterprises (SMEs) and women, as reflected by the low average implementation rates at 20% and 11%, respectively, indicating significant room for improvement in these areas.

Figure 1.8. Implementation of different groups of trade facilitation measures: Asia-Pacific average, 2017

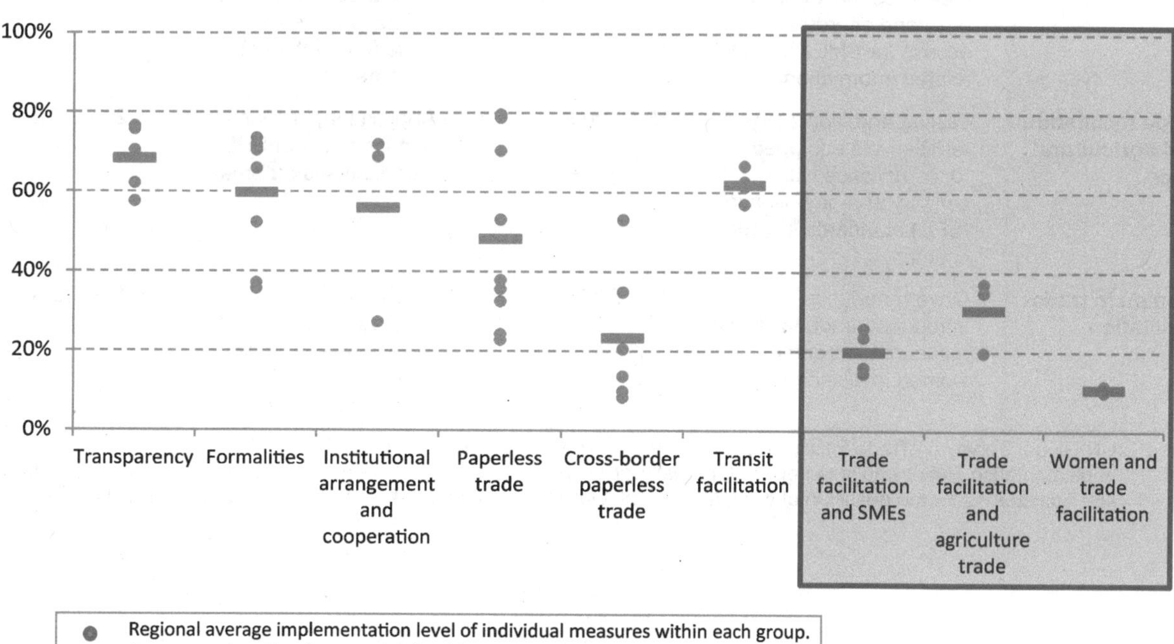

Source: UN Global Survey on Trade Facilitation and Paperless Trade Implementation, 2017

---

[9] UN-OHRLLS (2017). Vienna Programme of Action. Available from http://unohrlls.org/about-lldcs/programme-of-action/

Table 1.3. Most and least implemented measures in Asia-Pacific, 2017 (within each group of trade facilitation measures)

Category of trade facilitation measures	Most implemented (% of countries)		Least implemented (% of countries)	
	Measure	Implementation ratio*	Measure	Implementation ratio*
Transparency	Stakeholders' consultation on new draft regulations (prior to their finalization)	95.5 / 36.4	Advance ruling (on tariff classification)	68.2 / 36.4
Formalities	Risk management	93.2 / 38.6	Trade facilitation measures for authorized operators	45.5 / 20.5
Institutional arrangement and cooperation	National legislative framework and institutional arrangement are available to ensure border agencies to cooperate with each other	97.7 / 22.7	Government agencies delegating controls to Customs authorities	36.4 / 9.1
Paperless trade	Internet connection available to Customs and other trade control agencies at border-crossings	95.5 / 52.3	Electronic Application for Customs Refunds	29.5 / 9.1
Cross-border paperless trade	Laws and regulations for electronic transactions	72.7 / 15.9	Traders in your country apply for letters of credit electronically from banks or insurers without lodging paper-based documents	11.4 / 4.5
Transit facilitation	Transit facilitation agreement(s) with neighbouring country(ies)	56.8 / 2.3	Supporting pre-arrival processing for transit facilitation	40.9 / 11.4
Trade facilitation and SMEs	Government has developed trade facilitation measures that ensure easy and affordable access for SMEs to trade related information	36.4 / 9.1	Government has developed specific measures that enable SMEs to more easily benefit from the AEO scheme	20.5 / 11.4
Trade facilitation and agricultural trade	Testing and laboratory facilities are equipped for compliance with sanitary and phytosanitary (SPS) standards in your country	45.5 / 20.5	Application, verification and issuance of SPS certificates is automated	29.5 / 6.8
Women in trade facilitation	Government has introduced trade facilitation measures to benefit women involved in trade	18.2 / 2.3	The existing trade facilitation policy/strategy incorporates special consideration of women involved in trade	15.9 / 2.3

Source: UN Global Survey on Trade Facilitation and Paperless Trade Implementation, 2017
Note: Implementation Ratio: Implemented fully, partially or on pilot basis/Fully implemented (% of countries/% of countries) – see Annexes A2 for the definition of fully/partial or pilot implementation and A3 for further notes on calculation.

1.4.4. Progress in implementation between 2015 and 2017

Implementation rate of 31 common trade facilitation measures at the regional level increased by 5.6 percentage points from 44.8% in 2015 to 50.4% in 2017. The highest progress was observed in the North and Central Asia subregion: the implementation rate of the subregion increased by 10.2 percentage points (from 41.6% in 2015 to 51.8% in 2017). Substantial progress was observed in South and South-West Asia: the implementation rate of the subregion rose by 7.1 percentage points (from 39.4% in 2015 to 46.5% in 2017). Implementation rates of other subregions increased by 3 to 5 percentage points (figure 1.9).

Figure 1.9. Trade facilitation implementation by subregions in Asia and the Pacific, 2015 and 2017

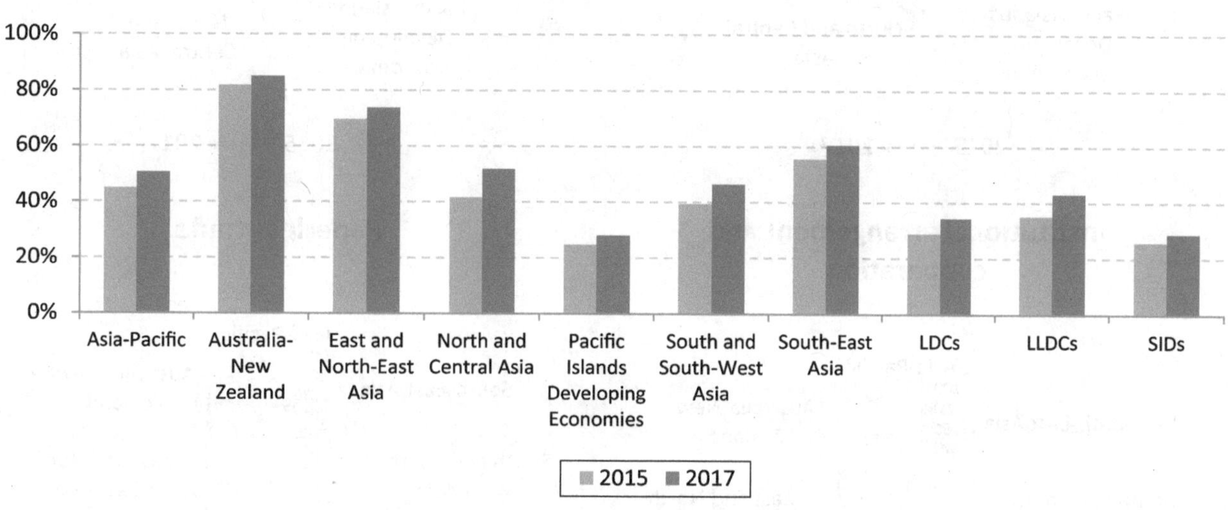

Source: UN Global Survey on Trade Facilitation and Paperless Trade Implementation, 2017

In terms of groups of trade facilitation measures, most progress was observed in "Institutional arrangement and cooperation": the implementation rate rose by 7.4 percentage points (from 48.7% in 2015 to 56.1% in 2017). Implementation rate of "Transparency" measures increased by 7 percentage points (from 61.5% in 2015 to 68.5% in 2017). Similarly, implementation rate of the "Formalities" measures improved by 7 percentage points (from 52.8% in 2015 to 59.8% in 2017). Implementation rates of both "paperless" and "cross-border paperless measures" rose by 4 percentage points between 2015 and 2017 (figures 1.10 and 1.11).

Figure 1.10. Implementation of different groups of trade facilitation measures in Asia-Pacific, 2015 and 2017

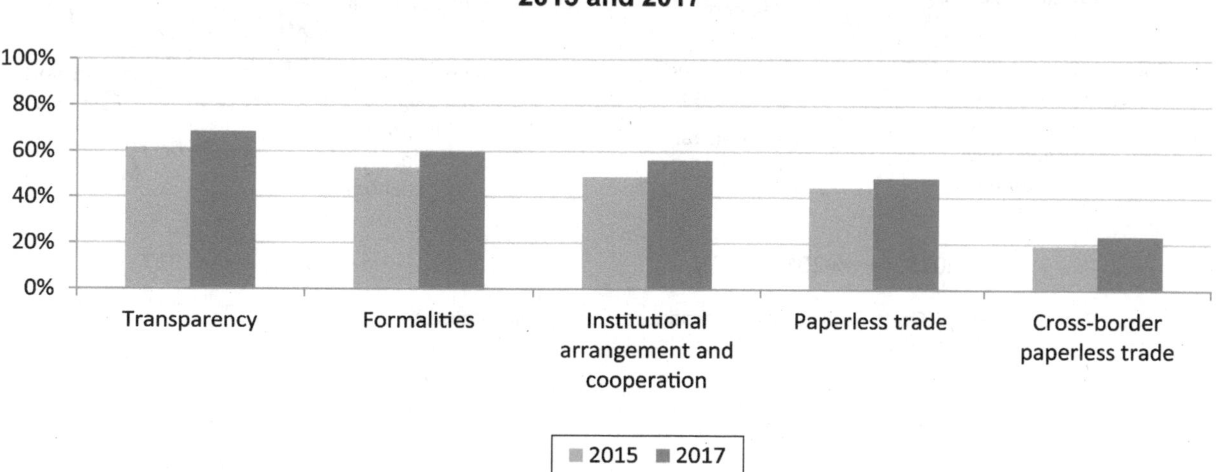

Source: UN Global Survey on Trade Facilitation and Paperless Trade Implementation, 2017

Figure 1.11. Implementation of trade facilitation measures by Asia-Pacific subregions, 2015 and 2017

Transparency

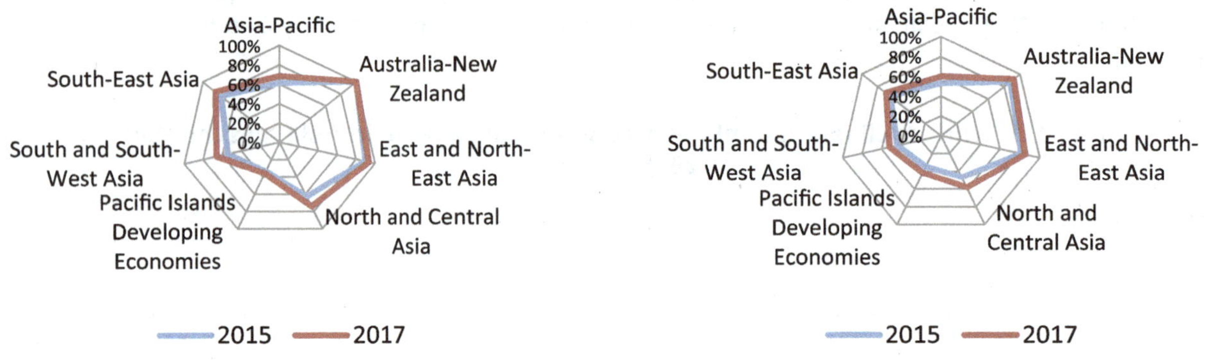

Formalities

Institutional arrangement and cooperation

Paperless trade

Cross-border paperless trade

Overall implementation

Source: UN Global Survey on Trade Facilitation and paperless Trade Implementation, 2017

1.5. Implementation of digital trade facilitation measures: A closer look

In this section, we review in more details the regional implementation of individual digital trade facilitation measures included in the UNTF Survey. Implementation of other trade facilitation measures included in the survey is discussed in ESCAP (2017b) – see also box 1.1 earlier in this chapter for implementation of measures related to specific WTO TFA articles.

1.5.1. "Paperless trade" measures

The regional and subregional average levels of implementation of the nine "paperless trade" measures vary widely. At the regional level, *Internet connection available to Customs and other trade control agencies at border-crossings* is among the most implemented measures of all trade facilitation measures included in the survey. The implementation levels of "paperless trade" measures in South-East Asia and East and North-East Asia exceed those in the other subregions, especially for *Electronic Single Window System*, *Electronic application and issuance of import and export permit* and *Electronic submission of Air Cargo Manifests*.

Recognizing the importance of having the basic ICT infrastructure and services in place to enable "paperless trade", nearly all countries (95%) have fully, partially, or on a pilot basis, made available *Internet connection to trade control agencies at border-crossings* (see figure 1.12). *Electronic/automated Customs System* is fully implemented in more than half of the countries of the region, and is in any case available at the main Customs station(s) in 41 out of 44 countries included in the survey. Similarly, *Electronic submission of customs declaration* has been fully or partially implemented by 17 and 21 countries, respectively. *Electronic Payment of customs duties and fees* is also at least partially available in most countries surveyed. *Electronic Single Window System* has been implemented fully, partially, or on a pilot basis by 23 countries, or more than 50% of all the Asia-Pacific countries surveyed (see box 1.2).

Figure 1.12. State of implementation of "paperless trade" measures in Asia-Pacific economies, 2017

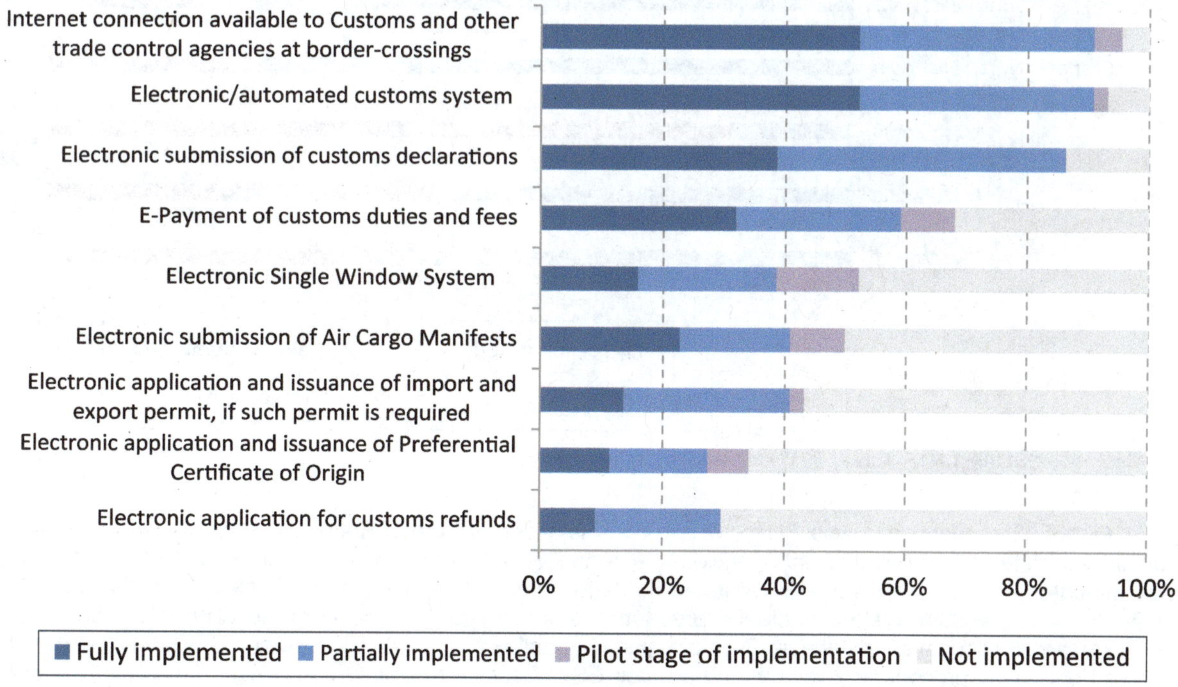

Source: UN Global Survey on Trade Facilitation and Paperless Trade Implementation, 2017

Some relatively simpler measures such as *Electronic application and issuance of import and export permit, Electronic application and Issuance of Preferential Certificate of Origin,* and *Electronic application for customs refunds* are even less implemented than *Single Window*. This could be partially explained by the fact that such agency-specific system may become redundant as single window systems are implemented. However, this also highlights that customs in most countries are indeed much more advanced than other trade-related agencies in developing and using electronic and automation system for trade facilitation and compliance.

Box 1.2. Electronic Single Window implementation in Asia and the Pacific

Single Window (SW) is arguably the most ambitions yet difficult to implement component of the WTO TFA. It is defined as a facility that allows parties involved in trade and transport to lodge standardized information and documents with a single entry point to fulfil all import, export, and transit-related regulatory requirements.[10] If information is electronic, then individual data elements should only be submitted once. An electronic single window (ESW) refers to a single window where data and documents are exchanged in electronic form.

Figure 1.13. reports the state of implementation of ESW in Asia-Pacific subregions in 2017. A large fraction of the economies surveyed in Pacific and South and South-West Asia subregions have yet to implement ESW systems. Indeed, of 13 economics in the Pacific, only two have "partially implemented" ESW. Of nine economies in South and South-West Asia, just three have "partially implemented" or are at the "planning stage" of ESW implementation. On the other hand, in South-East Asia subregion four countries out of 11 have 'fully implemented' ESW and just two are in "not implemented" stage. Overall, implementation rates in the Asia-Pacific remain below the global average.

Figure 1.13. State of implementation of ESW in Asia-Pacific subregions

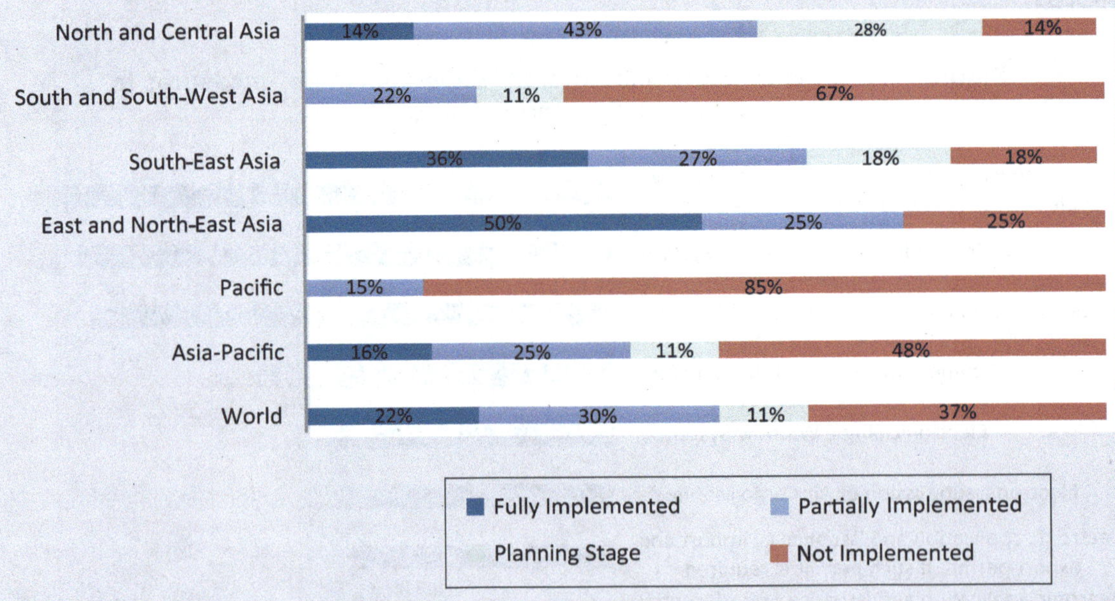

Source: ESCAP, UNTF Survey 2017.

Out of 23 economies in Asia-Pacific where ESW is at least at the pilot stage, 18 have a legal framework requiring all trade-related government agencies to use an ESW system. Similarly, around 53% of countries that have indicated at least pilot stage ESW implementation have already connected relevant trade facilitation stakeholders to the ESW system. Table 1.4 presents the implementation status of the various components of ESW in selected economies in the Asia-Pacific region. Republic of Korea, Singapore and Thailand use ESW for all seven paperless procedures, while the others use ESW for a more limited number of processes except for Malaysia and Indonesia where only one of the procedures is missing. Very limited or no information is available on Single Window functionalities in countries that have partially implemented ESW, indicating the difficulty in

---

[10] UN/CEFACT (2005). Recommendations and Guidelines on establishing a Single Window. Available from http://www.unece.org/fileadmin/DAM/cefact/recommendations/rec33/rec33_trd352e.pdf

actual access and use of the systems by the relevant stakeholders. In large economies such as China and India, ESW are often accessible and link agencies with each other, but these systems may not be not fully integrated or interconnected at the national level (e.g., no "national" ESW).

Table 1.4 Functionalities of SW in selected economies in Asia-Pacific

	Azer-baijan*	Brunei Darus-salam	India	Indo-nesia*	Japan*	Malay-sia*	New Zealand	Republic of Korea*	Singa-pore*	Thailand*
1. E-submission of customs declarations	√	√	√	√	√	√	√	√	√	√
2. E-Application and issuance of trade licences	√	X	X	√	√	√	–	√	√	√
3. E-submission of sea cargo manifests	X	√	√	√	√	√	X	√	√	√
4. E-submission of Air cargo manifests	X	√	√	√	–	√	√	√	√	√
5. E-application and issuance of Preferential Certificates of Origin	X	X	X	√	–	√	X	√	√	√
6. E-payment of customs duties and fees	√	X	X	√	√	√	X	√	√	√
7. E-Application for customs refunds	√	X	X	√	√	√	X	√	√	√

Note: √ = "Yes"; **X** = "No"; – = "NA".
Source: ESCAP, UNTF Survey 2017. * denotes economies that reported full SW implementation

1.5.2. "Cross-border paperless trade" measures

Among six "cross-border paperless trade" measures, two measures, *Laws and regulations for electronic transactions* and *Recognized certification authority,* are basic building blocks towards enabling the exchange and legal recognition of trade-related data and documents not only among stakeholders within a country, but ultimately also between stakeholders along the entire international supply chain. The other four measures relate to the implementation of systems enabling the actual exchange of trade-related data and documents across borders to remove the need for sending paper documents.

At the regional level, the implementation of these measures is very low, except *Laws and regulation for electronic transactions* whose implementation level is slightly over 50%. The pattern is very similar at the subregional level, apart from South-East Asia and East and North-East Asia whose implementation levels far exceed those of other subregions for most of the "cross-border paperless trade" measures.

Figure 1.14 shows that more than 70% of the countries surveyed in the Asia-Pacific have at least partially developed the legal and regulatory frameworks needed to support electronic transactions, but that these frameworks remain incomplete and may not readily support the legal recognition of electronic data or documents received from stakeholders in other countries. This is also true for Certification Authorities (CAs) needed to issue traders with recognized electronic signature certificates, which have yet to be established by a large majority of countries in the region even on a pilot basis.

Due to lack of institutional and legal frameworks to support cross-border paperless trade, *Engagement in trade-related cross-border electronic data exchange* has been typically conducted on a limited basis with a few specific trade partners, and often only on a partial or pilot implementation. Indeed, *Electronic exchange of Certificates of Origin* and *Electronic exchange of Sanitary & Phytosanitary Certificates* have been implemented on a limited basis by less than 30% of the economies of the region. Malaysia is one such country (see box 1.3).

Figure 1.14. State of implementation of "cross-border paperless trade" measures in Asia-Pacific economies, 2017

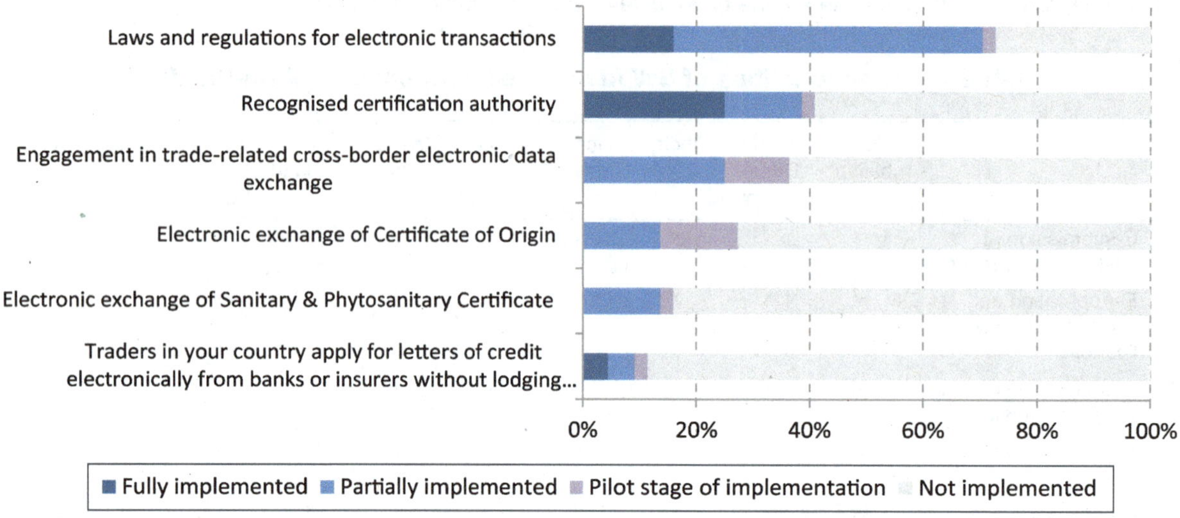

Source: UN Global Survey on Trade Facilitation and Paperless Trade Implementation, 2017

Box 1.3 The development of e-Certification of Agricultural Commodities in Malaysia

Electronic certification is an important means of facilitating agri-food trade. Complex global supply chains trade, advances in modes of transportation and increased trade volumes at entry points in the Asia-Pacific countries has increased the importance of electronic certification (or e-Cert). Implementation of e-Cert can help reduce forgery, increase transparency and enhance predictability in trade in agri-food products, and facilitate faster clearance at the entry points. In 2011, Malaysia initiated e-phytosanitary certification under its National Key Economic Area (NKEA) programme. The key objective of the NKEA programme is to stimulate a 20% increase in export of agricultural products and raise the nation's overall competitiveness.

E-phytosanitary certification, or MyPhyto as it is known in Malaysia, is a centralised system for the application and the issuance of phytosanitary certificates (PC) to certify pest-free and biologically safe agricultural products for export. Due to widely dispersed agriculture production areas and numerous exit points in Malaysia it was necessary to implement this centralised online system, in order to consolidate information from all of the Phytosanitary Certificate Issuance Offices (PCIO) and harmonise the operating procedures amongst them.

The MyPhyto online application for issuance of phytosanitary certificates has been successful in fulfilling the trade needs of Malaysia. Presently, the system generates between 70 and 90 thousand certificates a year and has reduced the issuance time from 4-8 days to less than 2 days. The system meets its objectives in centralizing information and data for real-time sharing and reporting. The system has also reduced face-to-face interactions and helped to harmonize the work flow. The implementation of the MyPhyto system has resulted in less forgery and greatly reduced instances of non-compliance to the importing countries. As a result, the clearance of agricultural commodities at entry points in Malaysia is much speedier, predictable and transparent.

The conversion to the online application of phytosanitary certificates has been fully implemented for all PCIOs in the country. However, printed versions of phytosanitary certificates are currently preferred by exporters due to the limited number of countries that have the online e-Phyto systems which support e-Cert exchange. The MyPhyto development team will explore more opportunities to initiate the discussion on e-Cert with major agricultural trading partners and may also request regional assistance to help with the negotiations. Work is also under way to integrate MyPhyto with the national single window system.

For more details on MyPhyto, as well as other case studies on digital trade facilitation in the agriculture sector, please see: https://unnext.unescap.org/policy-briefs

Source: UNNExT, Brief No. 19, March 2017.

1.6. Progress and challenges in the implementation

Figure 1.15 shows the top 10 trade facilitation measures on which countries made the most progress over the past 12 months. Several of these are digital trade facilitation measures.

Figure 1.15. Trade facilitation measures on which most progress was made in Asia-Pacific economies since 2016

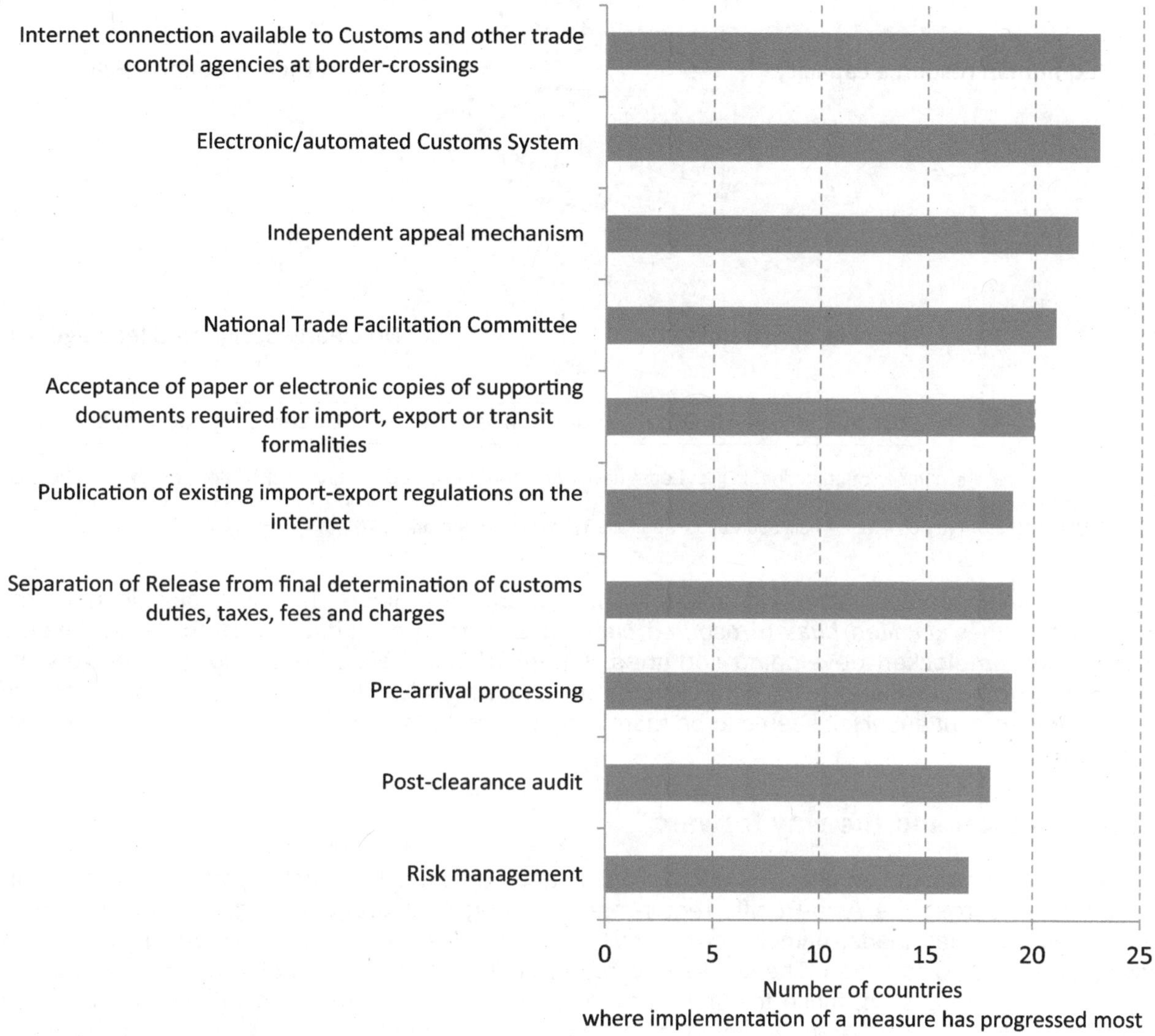

Source: UN Global Survey on Trade Facilitation and Paperless Trade Implementation, 2017

While the data remains anecdotal in nature, it suggests that many countries across the Asia-Pacific region prioritized improving their *Electronic/automated Customs System* and *Internet connection available to Customs and other trade control agencies at border-crossings* over the past year. Many also work on implementing *Independent appeal mechanism*, as well as *Establishing National Trade Facilitation Committee*. Finally, implementation of *Acceptance of paper or electronic copies of supporting documents required for import, export or transit formalities* also see significant progress.

Experts involved in the survey were also requested to identify the three key challenges faced by their countries in the implementation of trade facilitation measures. Responses were received for 20 countries. *Limited human resource capacity* and *Lack of coordination between government agencies* were identified as the most pressing challenges in 16 and 12 countries, respectively. Both *No clearly designated lead agency* and *Financial constraints* were mentioned in 11 countries.

Figure 1.16. Challenges faced by Asia-Pacific countries with special needs and other developing countries in implementing trade facilitation measures

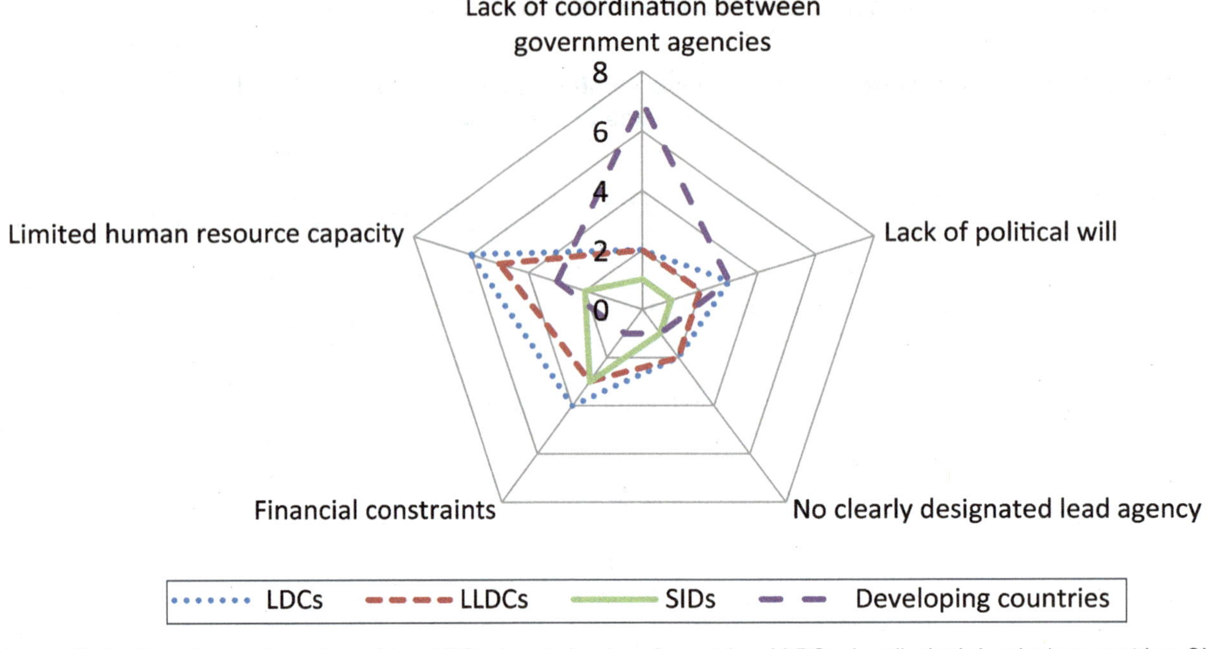

Note: Data show the number of countries. LDCs: Least developed countries; LLDCs: Landlocked developing countries; SIDs: Small island developing countries.

Source: UN Global Survey on Trade Facilitation and Paperless Trade Implementation, 2017

Five challenges associated with trade facilitation shown in figure 1.16 vary significantly across groups of countries. *Limited human resource capacity* seems to be most severe for least developed countries and landlocked developing countries, *Financial constraints* seems to be relatively more pertinent than other challenges for small islands developing states. In contrast, *Lack of coordination between Government agencies* seems to be more pronounced than other challenges in other developing countries.

1.7. Conclusion and the way forward

This chapter presented data on trade facilitation and paperless trade implementation collected from 44 economies across the Asia-Pacific region and covering 5 different subregions and 3 groups of countries with special needs, namely, least developed countries, landlocked developing countries and small islands developing states. The survey covered not only implementation of general trade facilitation measures, including most of those featured in the WTO TFA, but also more advanced ICT-based trade facilitation measures. Figure 1.17 confirms the strong relationship between Asia-Pacific countries international trade costs and their level of trade facilitation implementation.[11]

Based on a package of 31 trade facilitation measures included in the survey, regional average trade facilitation implementation is found to be approximately 50%, suggesting significant room for improvement. The assessment reveals that a large majority of countries in the region have been actively engaged in measures such as enhancing *Transparency*, strengthening *Institutional arrangements*, and streamlining *Formalities* associated with trade transactions. While Customs in essentially all countries have been actively developing paperless systems to speed up customs clearance while also improving control, more than 50% of the economies are now also engaged in implementation of more advanced national multi-agency paperless systems, such as national electronic single windows.

---

[11] A simple linear regression of trade costs against trade facilitation implementation – estimated using Ordinary Least Squares (OLS) – shows that trade facilitation implementation levels explain about 50% of the variations in trade costs; and that a 5% increase in the level of trade facilitation implementation is associated with a decrease in trade costs of 17%.

Figure 1.17. Trade facilitation implementation and Trade Costs of Asia-Pacific economies

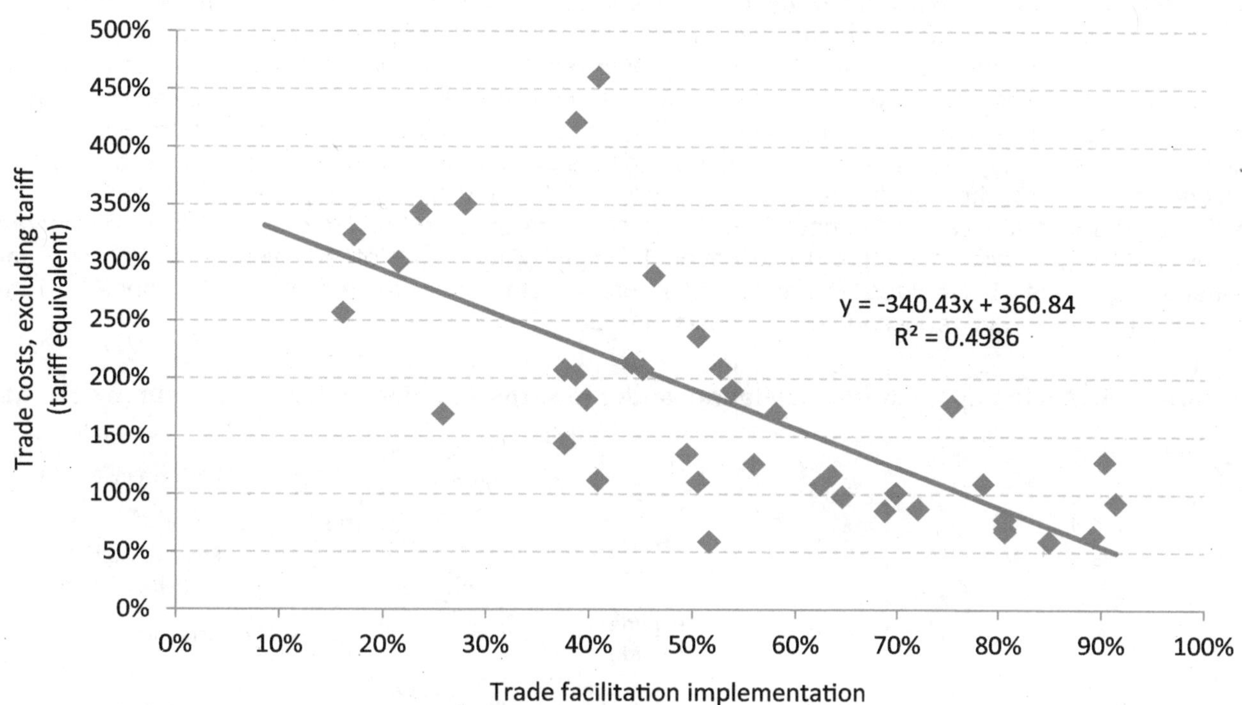

Notes: Countries' trade costs are based on average comprehensive bilateral trade costs with Germany, China and the USA (2008-13) and expressed as ad valorem equivalents (%).

Source: ESCAP-World Bank International Trade Cost Database (June 2017 Update) and UN Global Survey on Trade Facilitation and Paperless Trade Implementation, 2017

However, implementation of cross-border (bilateral, subregional or regional) paperless trade systems remains low. This is not surprising given that, on one hand, many less advanced countries in the region are at an early stage of development of national paperless systems and that, on the other hand, more advanced countries have paperless systems in place that are not fully interoperable with each other. In that regard, given the large potential benefits associated with the implementation of these "next generation" trade facilitation measures,[12] it is in the interest of countries from all groups to work together and develop the legal and technical protocols needed for the seamless exchange of regulatory and commercial data and documents along the international supply chain.

Some work has already been done bilaterally as well as in several Asian subregions (e.g., in ASEAN as part of implementation of the ASEAN Single Window). This work can be further leveraged at the regional level through adoption and implementation of the intergovernmental Framework Agreement for the Facilitation of Cross-border Paperless Trade. Negotiated as an inclusive and flexible intergovernmental platform to enable the electronic exchange of trade-related data and documents across borders among Parties, the Framework Agreement is set to benefit all parties regardless of their current state of implementation of paperless trade. Therefore, all countries in the region are encouraged to become a party of the treaty as soon as possible to take advantage of what the Agreement offers, especially in terms of accessing to capacity building and technical assistance.

Remarkably, the only trade facilitation performance "monitoring" measure included in the survey (*Establishment and publication of average release times*), has not been widely implemented across the region. This is worth highlighting, as what ultimately matters is not how many measures one implements, but how effective they have been in reducing the time and cost of trade transactions. Indeed, it is important to realize that trade facilitation and paperless trade measures are very much interrelated and that the effect of one particular measure on trade transaction costs depends on whether, and how well, other measures have been implemented.

---

[12]   Shepherd and Duval in ESCAP(2014) estimates that cross-border paperless trade facilitation in Asia and the Pacifc could generate over $250 billion in additional export potential. See http://www.unescap.org/resources/estimating-benefits-cross-border-paperless-trade

To achieve digital trade facilitation, figure 1.18 shows implementation as a step-by step process, based on the groups of measures included in this survey. Trade facilitation begins with the setting up of the *Institutional arrangement* needed to prioritize and coordinate implementation of trade facilitation measures. The next step is to make the trade processes more *Transparent* by sharing information on existing laws, regulations and procedures as widely as possible and consulting with stakeholders when developing new ones. Designing and implementing simpler and more efficient trade *Formalities* is the third step. The re-engineered and streamlined processes may first be implemented based on paper documents, but can then be further improved through ICT and the development of *Paperless trade* systems. The ultimate step is to enable the electronic trade data and documents exchange by traders, government and service providers within national (single window and other) systems to be used and re-used to provide stakeholders in partner countries with the information they need to speed up the movement of goods and reduce the overall costs of trade.[13]

Figure 1.18. Moving up the trade facilitation ladder towards seamless international supply chains

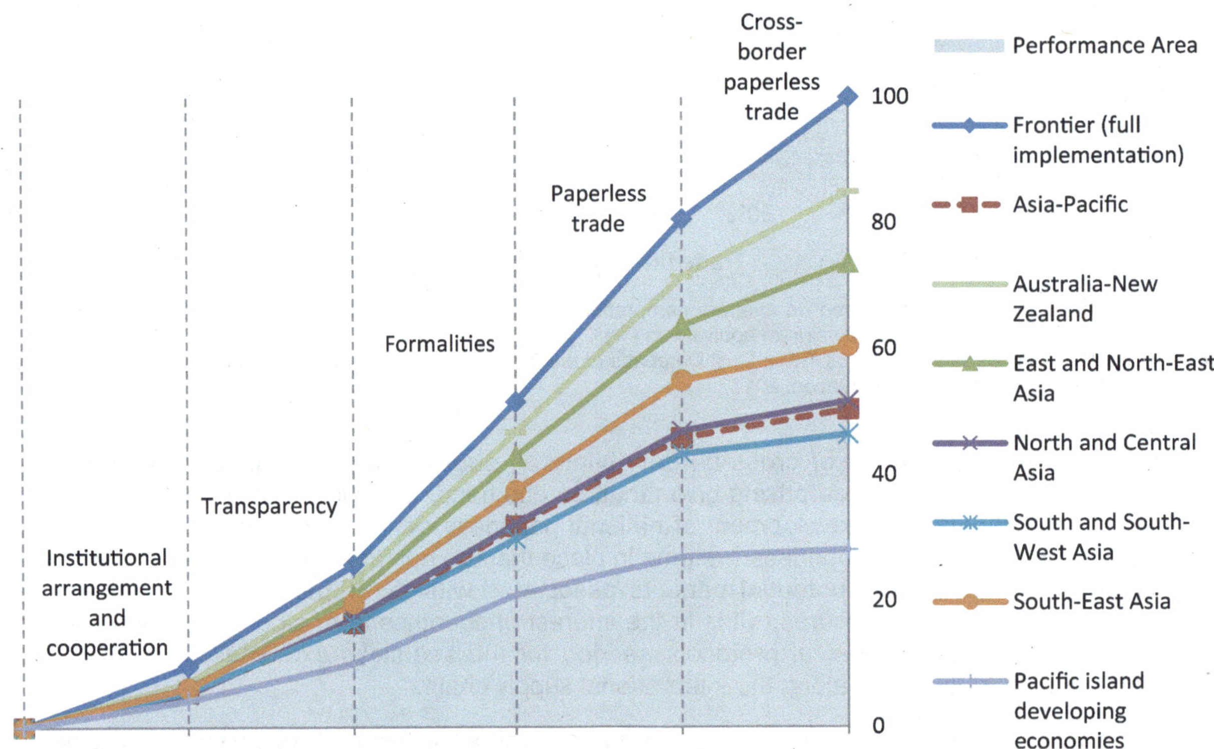

Note: The figure shows cumulative trade facilitation implementation scores of Asia-Pacific subregions for 31 common trade facilitation measures included in the survey. Full implementation of all measures = 100.

Source: UN Global Survey on Trade Facilitation and Paperless Trade Implementation, 2017

Going forward, digital trade facilitation offers a great opportunity to reduce trade costs and increase trade volume for the region. Through paperless trade and seamless electronic exchange of trade data and documents, member countries can enhance their competitiveness in global markets and increase more effective participation in global value chains. In this respect, the *Framework Agreement on Facilitation of Cross-Border Paperless Trade in Asia and the Pacific* does not only complement the WTO TFA but also provides a unique platform for ESCAP member States to tap their potential (see chapter 4 in this publication). In the context of 2030 Agenda for Sustainable Development, member States should also introduce and implement new trade facilitation measures that incorporate inclusiveness and sustainability, especially the ones that benefit SMEs and the agricultural sector, as well as the participation of women in trade.

---

[13] This step-by-step process is inspired from and generally consistent with the UN/CEFACT step-by-step approach to trade facilitation towards a single window environment.

References

Arvis, J. F., Duval, Y., Shepherd, B., and Utoktham, C. (2013). Trade Costs in the Developing World: 1995-2010. World Bank Policy Research Working Paper No. 6309.

ESCAP (2017). Asia-Pacific Trade and Investment Report 2017: Channelling Trade and Investment into Sustainable Development. Chapter 6: The impacts of trade and complementary policy changes on sustainable development. Available at: http://www.unescap.org/publications/APTIR2017

ESCAP (2017b). Trade Facilitation and Paperless Trade Implementation in Asia and the Pacific – Regional Report 2017. Available at: http://www.unescap.org/resources/trade-facilitation-and-paperless-trade-implementation-asia-and-pacific-regional-report

UNNExT (2017). Electronic Phytosanitary Certificates for Agricultural Commodities in Malaysia, Brief No. 19, March 2017. Available at: http://www.unescap.org/resources/unnext-brief-no-19-electronic-phytosanitary-certificates-agricultural-commodities-malaysia

Annex

A1. Grouping of the countries surveyed[14]

The survey covers 44 Asia-Pacific countries, which can be divided into the following six subregions:

- *East and North-East Asia* (ENEA): China, Japan, Mongolia and Republic of Korea;
- *North and Central Asia (*NCA): Armenia, Azerbaijan, Kazakhstan, Kyrgyzstan, the Russian Federation, Tajikistan and Uzbekistan;
- *Pacific Island Developing Economies* (PIDEs): Fiji, Kiribati, Micronesia, Nauru, Palau, Papua New Guinea, Samoa, Solomon Islands, Tonga, Tuvalu and Vanuatu;
- *South and South-West Asia* (SSWA): Afghanistan, Bangladesh, Bhutan, India, Maldives, Nepal, Pakistan, Sri Lanka and Turkey;
- *Pacific developed countries* (AU&NZ): Australia and New Zealand;
- *South-East Asia* (SEA) Brunei Darussalam, Cambodia, Indonesia, the Lao People's Democratic Republic, Malaysia, Myanmar, Philippines, Singapore, Thailand, Timor-Leste and Viet Nam.

Analysis is also extended to the following group of countries with special needs: [15]

- *Least developed countries*: Afghanistan, Bangladesh, Bhutan, Cambodia, Kiribati, Lao PDR, Myanmar, Nepal, Solomon Islands, Timor-Leste, Tuvalu and Vanuatu;
- *Landlocked developing countries*: Afghanistan, Armenia, Azerbaijan, Bhutan, Kazakhstan, Kyrgyzstan, Lao PDR, Mongolia, Nepal, Tajikistan and Uzbekistan;
- *Small island developing states*: Fiji, Kiribati, Maldives, Micronesia, Nauru, Palau, Papua New Guinea, Samoa, Solomon Islands, Timor-Leste, Tonga, Tuvalu and Vanuatu.[16]

---

[14] This grouping is largely in line with the Economic and Social Survey of Asia and the Pacific 2015.

[15] More details are available at http://unohrlls.org/UserFiles/1_countries_with_special_needs.pdf.

[16] It is important to note that Afghanistan, Bhutan and the Lao People's Democratic Republic are both least developed and landlocked countries, while Kiribati, Solomon Islands, Timor-Leste, Tuvalu and Vanuatu are both least developed and small island developing states.

A2. Definition of the different stages of implementation

Definition of stage of implementation	Coding/ Scoring
Full implementation: the trade facilitation measure implemented is in full compliance with commonly accepted international standards, recommendations and conventions (such as the Revised Kyoto Convention, UN/CEFACT Recommendations, or the WTO Trade Facilitation Agreement); it is implemented in law and in practice; it is available to essentially all relevant stakeholders nationwide, supported by adequate legal and institutional framework, as well as adequate infrastructure and financial and human resources.	3
Partial implementation: a measure is considered to be partially implemented if at least one of the following is true: (1) the trade facilitation measure is not in full compliance with commonly accepted international standards, recommendations and conventions; (2) the country is still in the process of rolling out the implementation of measure; (3) the measure is practiced on an unsustainable, short-term or ad-hoc basis; (4) the measure is not implemented in all targeted locations (such as key border crossing stations); or (5) not all targeted stakeholders are fully involved.	2
Pilot stage of implementation: A measure is considered to be at the pilot stage of implementation if, in addition to meeting the general attributes of partial implementation, it is available only to (or at) a very small portion of the intended stakeholder group (location) and/or is being implemented on a trial basis. When a new trade facilitation measure is under pilot stage of implementation, the old measure is often continuously used in parallel to ensure the service is provided in case of disruption of new measure. This stage of implementation also includes relevant rehearsals and preparation for the full-fledged implementation.	1
Not implemented: simply means a trade facilitation measure has not been implemented. However, this stage does not rule out initiatives or efforts towards implementation of the measure. For example, under this stage, (pre)feasibility or planning of implementation can be carried out; and consultation with stakeholders on the implementation may be arranged.	0

A3. Explanatory notes

1. Any missing data or "don't know" (DK) answer is included in the "not implemented" category when presenting aggregate results at the global/regional/subregional levels.

2. "Not applicable" (NA) was accepted as an answer for the following measures as geographical factors may not permit a country to implement such measures:

    Measure 20:   Electronic Submission of Sea Cargo Manifests

    Measure 33:   Alignment of working days and hours with neighbouring countries at border crossings

    Measure 34:   Alignment of formalities and procedures with neighbouring countries at border crossings

    Measure 35:   Transit facilitation agreement(s) with neighbouring country(ies)

    Measure 36:   Customs Authorities limit the physical inspections of transit goods and use risk assessment

    Measure 37:   Supporting pre-arrival processing for transit facilitation

    Measure 38:   Cooperation between agencies of countries involved in transit

    In calculating overall implementation rate of a country, the above-mentioned measures were excluded. Furthermore, measures 39-47 were excluded for calculating the overall implementation rate of a country due to incompleteness of the dataset.

3. ESCAP dataset was finalized on 12 August 2017.

Chapter 2

Impact of digital trade facilitation on trade costs

2.1. Introduction

As noted in the previous chapter, developing economies are especially susceptible to high trade costs. Reduction of trade costs in developing countries would encourage their greater participation in international trade, boost trade flows and contribute to their economic development. A wide consensus exists in the literature that future reductions in trade costs will come from addressing non-tariff barriers (NTBs) to trade, including through digital trade facilitation. Digital trade facilitation through cross-border paperless trade measures implementation discussed in the previous chapter thus holds promise to further bring down trade costs and enhance trade. To demonstrate the potential benefits of digital trade facilitation, this chapter seeks to quantify the impact of various levels of trade facilitation measures implementation on trade costs.

This study uses the detailed data from the UN Global Survey on Trade Facilitation and Paperless Trade Implementation (UNTF Survey). The effects of implementation of measures featured in the WTO TFA as well as more advanced paperless trade measures outside the scope of the WTO TFA are examined. The findings suggest that digital trade facilitation implementation, such as through the Framework Agreement on Facilitation of Cross-border Paperless Trade in Asia and the Pacific, can double the benefits of a narrower WTO TFA implementation.[1]

The study further estimates the impact on trade costs of a country due to own trade facilitation measures implementation as well as due to trade partners' implementation. The results suggest that implementation of trade facilitation measures by trade partners can also significantly reduce a country's own trade costs. As such, to reduce trade costs and boost trade the governments should actively collaborate, particularly on paperless cross-border trade facilitation initiatives, even if their own countries' trade facilitation measures implementation rates are already high.

This chapter is structured as follows. Data and methodology for the study, including a summary of trade facilitation implementation levels in Asia and the Pacific, are presented in the next section. Results of the estimation of trade costs models follow in section 3. Counterfactual assessments of the trade cost reductions associated with a country's own trade facilitation reforms and/or those undertaken by its trade partners, are analysed in section 4. Section 5 concludes and presents the way forward for Asia and the Pacific.

2.2. Trade facilitation implementation and trade costs: data description and methodology

Building on the inverse gravity approach pioneered by Novy (2013), several studies inferred aggregate trade costs from gross trade and output data, and set out to directly measure the contribution of tariffs and NTBs on such comprehensive trade costs. Regional analysis in Asia and the Pacific by ESCAP, 2015, found that while tariff costs accounted for 2-3% of trade costs across countries, natural trade costs such as geography (i.e., distance, landlockedness etc.), cultural distance and historical relationships (i.e., language, colonization etc.) between countries accounted for an additional 20-21% of trade costs. More importantly, policy-related NTBs accounted for the remaining 76-78% of trade costs. The study found that international trade costs in that broad category were affected by liner shipping (maritime) connectivity, the domestic business environment of the trading partners, the availability and use of ICT services, the direct cost of trade procedures as well as by other policy related factors – the effect of which was difficult to disentangle, given the lack of data.

---

[1] ADB and ESCAP (2017) finds similar results. See also ESCAP (2015) and OECD (2015).

To assess the effect of trade facilitation implementation on trade costs, this study first outlines the trade cost model and estimation methods used. Next, trade facilitation implementation indicators and data used in the estimation are introduced.

2.2.1. Trade costs model estimation

In line with previous studies (see Arvis et al., 2013), trade costs can be modelled as a function of natural geographic factors (i.e., distance, landlockedness and contiguity), cultural and historical distance (i.e. common official language, common unofficial language, former colonial relationships and formerly same country), the presence of regional trade agreements and liner shipping connectivity. The trade cost models estimated here also include trade facilitation implementation indicators, as well as an index of credit information capturing the impact on trade costs of domestic access to credit and cost of financial services – as such factor was identified as significant in earlier work (e.g., ESCAP, 2015).

In order to better understand the impact on trade cost of a country's own implementation of trade facilitation reform, and that resulting from trade facilitation improvements in partner countries, two trade cost models are specified as follows:

Model I: Trade cost model with average trade facilitation (TF) implementation in own country and trading partner

$$\ln(\tau_{ij}) = \beta_0 + \beta_1 \ln(gtariff_{ij}) + \beta_2 \ln(dist_{ij}) + \beta_3(contig_{ij}) + \beta_4(comlang\_off_{ij}) + \beta_5(comlang\_ethno_{ij}) + \beta_6(colony_{ij})$$
$$+ \beta_7(comcol_{ij}) + \beta_8(smctry_{ij}) + \beta_9(rta_{ij}) + \beta_{10}(landlocked_{ij}) + \beta_{11} \ln(creditindex_{ij}) + \beta_{12} \ln(LSCI_{ij})$$
$$+ \beta_{13} \ln(TF_{ij}) + D_i + D_j + \varepsilon_{ij}$$

Model II: Trade cost model with separate TF implementation in own country and trading partner

$$\ln(\tau_{ij}) = \beta_0 + \beta_1 \ln(gtariff_{ij}) + \beta_2 \ln(dist_{ij}) + \beta_3(contig_{ij}) + \beta_4(comlang\_off_{ij}) + \beta_5(comlang\_ethno_{ij}) + \beta_6(colony_{ij})$$
$$+ \beta_7(comcol_{ij}) + \beta_8(smctry_{ij}) + \beta_9(rta_{ij}) + \beta_{10}(landlocked_{ij}) + \beta_{14} \ln(creditindex_i) + \beta_{15} \ln(LSCI_i)$$
$$+ \beta_{16} \ln(TF_i) + \beta_{17} \ln(creditindex_j) + \beta_{18} \ln(LSCI_j) + \beta_{19} \ln(TF_j) + D_i + D_j + \varepsilon_{ij}$$

These two models extend the model featured in ESCAP (2015), which only captured the impact of own country trade facilitation reform implementation. Variables, their definitions, treatment, sources and expected signs used in estimation are summarized in table 2.1. Fixed-effects dummy variables for income groups (D_i and D_j) are included in order to account for cross-group heterogeneity as well as to increase estimation efficiency.[2] Robust standard errors are clustered by country pairs. The model is estimated using ordinary least square across a cross-section of 96 reporting countries. The list of reporting and partner countries included in the estimation is available in Duval et al. (2018).

---

[2] The same set of fixed effects are used in model I and II to make the results across models more comparable. However, in line with the structural gravity literature, we also estimate model I using full country fixed effects, which yields similar and generally statistically significant results as well. See Annex of Duval et al. (2018) for details.

Table 2.1. Variables, definitions, treatments, sources and expected signs

Variable	Definition	Data Treatment	Source	Expected Sign
τ_{ij}	Comprehensive trade costs.	Average of 2013-2015	World Bank -ESCAP Trade Cost Database	N/A
$gtariff_{ij}$	Geometric average tariff factor (1+rate) that each reporting country (i) charges to its trade partner (j) and vice versa, which can be expressed as $gtariff_{ij} = \sqrt{tariff_{ij} \times tariff_{ij}}$	Average of 2013-2015	World Integrated Trade Solution (WITS)	+
$dist_{ij}$	Geographical distance between country i and j.	N/A	CEPII	+
$contig_{ij}$	1 if country i and j share a common border and zero otherwise.	N/A	CEPII	–
$comlang\_off_{ij}$	1 if country i and j use the same common official language and zero otherwise.	N/A	CEPII	–
$comlang\_ethno_{ij}$	1 if a language is spoken by at least 9% of the population in both countries and zero otherwise.	N/A	CEPII	–
$colony_{ij}$	1 if country i and j were ever in colonial relationship and zero otherwise.	N/A	CEPII	–
$comcol_{ij}$	1 if country i and j had a common colonizer after 1945 and zero otherwise.	N/A	CEPII	–
$smctry_{ij}$	1 if country i and j were or are the same country and zero otherwise.	N/A	CEPII	–
rta_{ij}	1 if country i and j are members of the same regional trade agreement and zero otherwise.	Latest definition in 2015	De Sousa, J. (2012)	–
$landlocked_{ij}$	1 if either country i or j is landlocked and zero otherwise.	N/A	CEPII	+
$creditindex_i /$ $creditindex_j /$ $creditindex_{ij}$	Average depth of credit information index of country, i, j and geometric average of i and j [3]	0.0001 replacement/ average of DB2014-2016	Doing Business	–
$LSCI_i /$ $LSCI_j /$ $LSCI_{ij}$	Average scores of liner shipping connectivity index of country i, j and geometric average of i and j	Data filling/average of 2013-2015	UNCTAD	–
$TF_i /$ $TF_j /$ TF_{ij}	Percentage of TF implementation of country i, j and geometric average of i and j modelled as: (a) overall TF and; (b) general TF and (paperless + cross-border paperless trade) [4]	0.0001 replacement data in 2015	Global Survey on Trade Facilitation and Paperless Trade Implementation: 2017	–

Note: Where available, the average of the most recent data in 2013-2015 is used in the estimation. Data filling for LSCI is required to ensure inclusion of landlocked economies. Port countries are used as proxies for landlocked countries' portal performance. For the TF components and credit information index, zeros are replaced by 0.0001 to prevent observations being omitted from the estimation.

---

[3] Data for credit information from the Doing Business Report is lagged one year, i.e., data from the Doing Business Report 2014 are from 2013. Geometric average of credit information index is defined as $creditindex_{ij} = \sqrt{creditindex_i \times creditindex_j}$. Geometric average formula also applies to $LSCI_{ij}$ and TF_{ij}

[4] See scoring of different stages of implementation see Annex A2 from Chapter 1 on page 25.

2.2.2. Overview of data on trade facilitation implementation

The impact of trade facilitation on trade costs is captured in the model by including trade facilitation implementation rates calculated on the basis of the United Nations Global Survey on Trade Facilitation and Paperless Trade Implementation (UNTF Survey).[5] This survey provides data on the implementation of a range of TF measures related to the WTO TFA as well as more advanced digital trade facilitation measures, as discussed in the previous chapter.[6] The list of measures and the groupings considered in the calculation of aggregate implementation rates are shown in the previous chapter in table 1.2 on (page 15).[7] General TF measures are all directly related to various WTO TFA provisions. In contrast, most paperless and cross-border paperless trade measures are not specifically included in the WTO TFA, and their implementation goes beyond the binding commitments made under the Agreement.

Trade facilitation implementation rates for 2017 are shown in figure 2.1a. Global average rate of implementation is approximately 60%. There is significant cross-regional heterogeneity in the rates of implementation, which range from an average of 52% in Sub-Saharan Africa to almost 80% in the developed economies. In most cases, high income economies generally have higher trade facilitation implementation rates than other economies. Landlocked, least developed and small island developing states tend to lag behind. This is highlighted by figure 2.1b, which shows the implementation rates across the Asia-Pacific subregions.

Figure 2.1. Trade facilitation implementation rate

2.1a. Rates of implementation in major regions

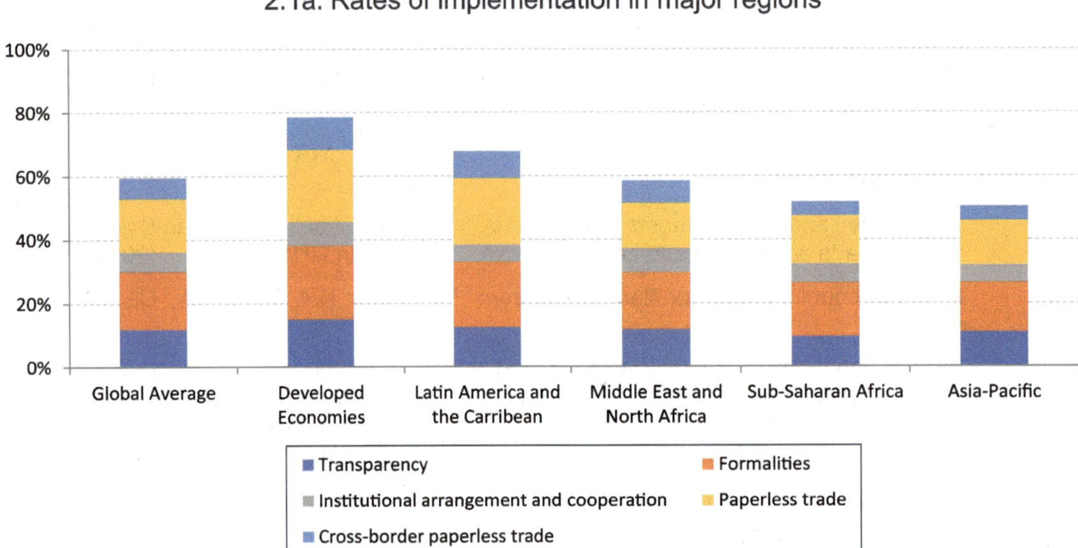

---

[5] UNTF Survey Dataset is updated as of August 2017.

[6] Implementation of each measure is rated as "fully", "partially", "on a pilot basis" or "not" implemented (see Table A1.2 in Annex 1 for more details). More information and survey methodology and data are available at http://unnext.unescap.org/UNTFSurvey2017.asp.

[7] For each country, the UNTF Survey features data on up to 38 trade facilitation measures. However, not all measures are applicable to all countries (e.g., transit facilitation measures), and data is missing for some of the more advanced measures in some countries. In order to ensure that the trade cost model estimation can be made on the basis of a sufficiently large number of countries, implementation rates are calculated on the basis of a common set of 31 trade facilitation measures in "General trade facilitation", paperless trade and cross-border paperless trade measures only (excluding Question 20, 33, and 34).

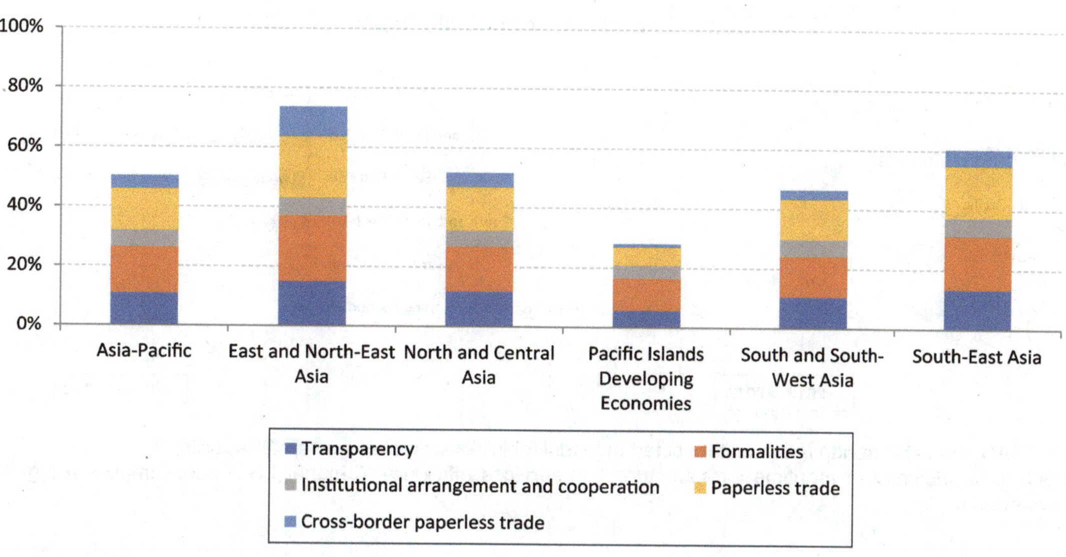

2.1b. Subregional implementation rates in Asia and the Pacific

Source: Authors' compilation, based on the UNTF Survey 2017.
Note: *Based on implementation rates of 31 of 38 main individual trade facilitation measures included in the UNTF Survey. Implementation of transit facilitation, trade facilitation and SMEs, trade facilitation and agricultural trade and women and trade facilitation are not included.

As efforts in reducing trade costs are not limited to the implementation of customs and information and data exchange facilitation measures as featured in the WTO TFA, streamlining other trade-related procedures (e.g., transport and payment procedures) and improvement of trade-related infrastructure for goods and services should also be considered when modelling trade costs. The United Nations Conference on Trade and Development (UNCTAD) Liner Shipping Connectivity Index (LSCI) and the World Bank Doing Business Credit Information Index (CII) are therefore included in the trade cost models featured in this study to capture broader aspects of trade facilitation.[8]

Figure 2.2 shows that the Asia-Pacific region performs moderately well in terms of both maritime connectivity (see figure 2.2a) and financing environment (see figure 2.2b). Asia-Pacific's top performer is East and North-East Asia subregion, with Pacific island developing economies consistently and significantly lagging behind other Asia-Pacific subregions, particularly in terms of liner shipping connectivity.

2.3. Results

Outputs from cross-sectional fixed effects regressions are presented in table 2.2.[9] The trade cost models I and II introduced earlier are estimated using two different specifications of trade facilitation: Model (I.1) and (II.1) are estimated using overall trade facilitation implementation rate across all relevant trade facilitation and paperless trade measures in the UNTF Survey; Model (I.2) and (II.2) features disaggregated trade facilitation implementation rates, distinguishing between implementation of general trade facilitation measures (i.e., WTO TFA measures) and implementation of digital trade facilitation measures (paperless trade and cross-border paperless trade measures in the UNTF Survey).

All the estimated statistically significant coefficients have expected signs in every model. Distance ($dist_{ij}$) and landlockedness ($landlocked_{ij}$) all increase trade costs significantly. Having a common border ($contig_{ij}$), a common official language ($comlang\_off_{ij}$), being part of the same RTA (rta_{ij}), having a former common colonizer ($comcol_{ij}$) and/or a former colonial relationship ($colony_{ij}$), and having formerly belonged to the same country ($smctry_{ij}$) are all associated with statistically significant and lower bilateral trade costs. Having a common unofficial ($comlang\_ethno_{ij}$) language is not found to be statistically significant.

---

[8] WTO 2015

[9] Refer back to table 2.1 for the definitions of variables.

Figure 2.2. Selected broad trade facilitation indicators

2.2a. Liner Shipping Connectivity Index (LSCI)

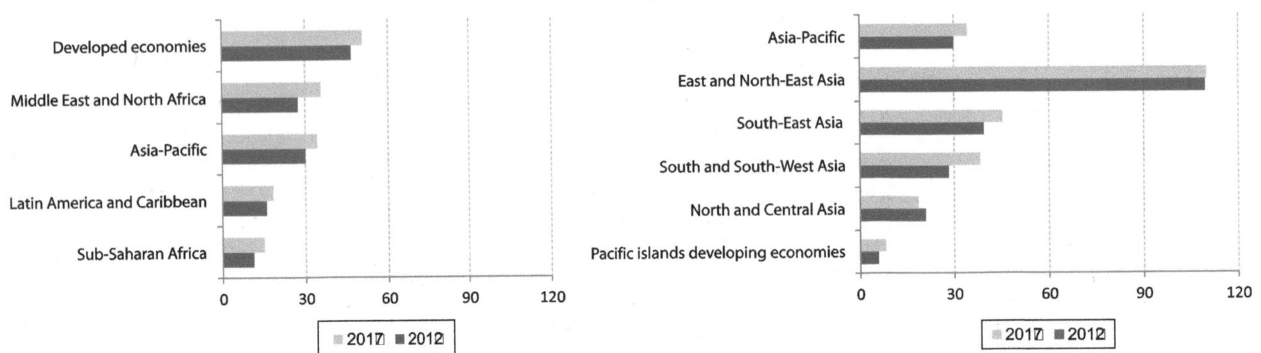

Source: UNCTAD, available at http://unctadstat.unctad.org/wds/TableViewer/tableView.aspx?ReportId=92
Note: LSCI is an indicator of maritime infrastructure and services efficiency. A higher LSCI score implies a higher maritime connectivity.

2.2b. Credit Information Index (CII)

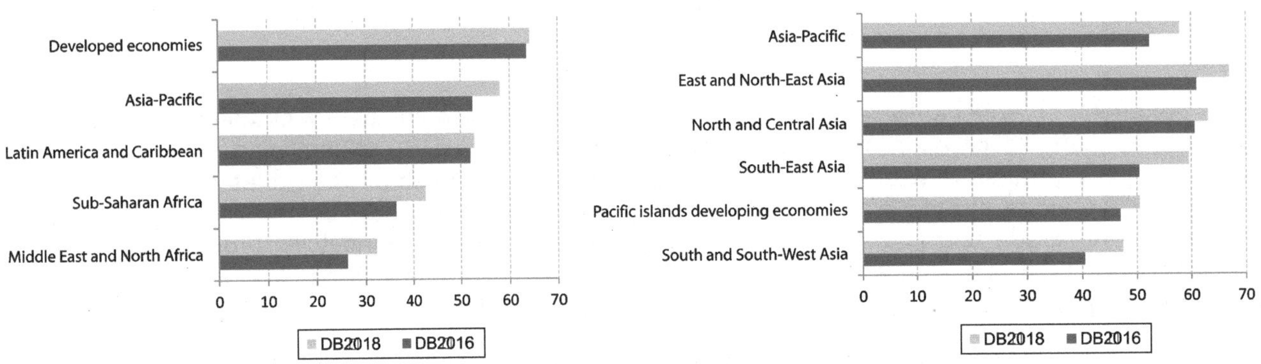

Source: World Bank Doing Business Report, available at www.doingbusiness.org.
Note: CII is one of the World Bank indicators of ease of financing in the World Bank Doing Business Report. CII scores range from 0 to 100. Higher scores indicate higher access and quality of credit information, contributing to a better environment for financing transactions.

In terms of policy and infrastructure factors related to trade facilitation, maritime connectivity ($LSCI_{ij}$), and ease of financing and trade facilitation implementation ($creditindex_{ij}$) indicators both have the expected and statistically significant negative impact on trade costs. Although efforts on tariff reductions have been encouraged during the past two decades, further reducing them globally remains an effective way to reduce trade costs. Results across all four models suggest that a 10%[10] change in tariffs ($gtariff_{ij}$) may be expected to reduce overall trade costs by approximately 3%, on average.

The main variables of interest in this study are trade facilitation implementation variables (*TF*). The results emphasize the importance of trade facilitation implementation, with a 10% increase in the overall implementation of trade facilitation measures (*Overall TF_{ij}*) associated with a 4.6% reduction in trade costs – see Model (I.1).

---

[10] All percentage signs (%) mean a percentage changes, unless stated otherwise.

Table 2.2. Trade costs model reults

Dependent variable: τ_{ij} / Independent variables:	Beta coefficients				Standardized beta			
	MODEL I		MODEL II		MODEL I		MODEL II	
	(I.1) overall TFI	(I.2) gen+dig TF	(II.1) overall TFI	(II.2) gen+dig TF	(I.2) overall TFI	(I.2) gen+dig TFI	(II.1) overall TFI	(II.2) gen+dig TFI
log($gtariff_{ij}$)	0.290* [1.766]	0.273* [1.656]	0.336** [2.068]	0.322** [1.996]	0.0316* [1.766]	0.0297* [1.656]	0.0366** [2.068]	0.0350** [1.996]
log($dist_{ij}$)	0.174*** [22.59]	0.171*** [22.12]	0.172*** [22.58]	0.171*** [22.29]	0.342*** [22.59]	0.336*** [22.12]	0.340*** [22.58]	0.338*** [22.29]
$contig_{ij}$	-0.165*** [-5.034]	-0.169*** [-5.171]	-0.167*** [-5.188]	-0.168*** [-5.256]	-0.0711*** [-5.034]	-0.0728*** [-5.171]	-0.0720*** [-5.188]	-0.0723*** [-5.256]
$comlang\_off_{ij}$	-0.0757*** [-2.801]	-0.0764*** [-2.801]	-0.0797*** [-2.914]	-0.0827*** [-3.027]	-0.0660*** [-2.801]	-0.0666*** [-2.801]	-0.0695*** [-2.914]	-0.0721*** [-3.027]
$comlang\_ethno_{ij}$	0.0265 [1.068]	0.0241 [0.963]	0.0297 [1.178]	0.0323 [1.286]	0.0241 [1.068]	0.0219 [0.963]	0.0270 [1.178]	0.0294 [1.286]
$colony_{ij}$	-0.143*** [-3.789]	-0.142*** [-3.763]	-0.138*** [-3.635]	-0.140*** [-3.687]	-0.0464*** [-3.789]	-0.0460*** [-3.763]	-0.0448*** [-3.635]	-0.0451*** [-3.687]
$comcol_{ij}$	-0.0399** [-2.034]	-0.0367* [-1.866]	-0.0404** [-2.074]	-0.0384** [-1.963]	-0.0297** [-2.034]	-0.0273* [-1.866]	-0.0301** [-2.074]	-0.0286** [-1.963]
$smctry_{ij}$	-0.124*** [-2.765]	-0.129*** [-2.890]	-0.126*** [-2.844]	-0.128*** [-2.921]	-0.0353*** [-2.765]	-0.0368*** [-2.890]	-0.0359*** [-2.844]	-0.0367*** [-2.921]
$landlocked_{ij}$	0.277*** [20.43]	0.277*** [20.29]	0.276*** [20.63]	0.278*** [20.60]	0.319*** [20.43]	0.319*** [20.29]	0.317*** [20.63]	0.320*** [20.60]
rta_{ij}	-0.0882*** [-6.203]	-0.0907*** [-6.360]	-0.0871*** [-6.160]	-0.0881*** [-6.254]	-0.0912*** [-6.203]	-0.0938*** [-6.360]	-0.0901*** [-6.160]	-0.0911*** [-6.254]
log($creditindex_{ij}$)	-0.0770*** [-5.260]	-0.0795*** [-5.421]			-0.0681*** [-5.260]	-0.0704*** [-5.421]		
log($creditindex_{i}$)			-0.0671*** [-7.594]	-0.0657*** [-7.417]			-0.0924*** [-7.594]	-0.0904*** [-7.417]
log($creditindex_{j}$)			0.00334 [0.263]	-0.00285 [-0.223]			0.00375 [0.263]	-0.00320 [-0.223]
log($LSCI_{ij}$)	-0.228*** [-22.40]	-0.229*** [-22.32]			-0.344*** [-22.40]	-0.344*** [-22.32]		
log($LSCI_{i}$)			-0.0946*** [-13.90]	-0.0959*** [-14.02]			-0.212*** [-13.90]	-0.215*** [-14.02]
log($LSCI_{j}$)			-0.135*** [-19.28]	-0.135*** [-19.20]			-0.288*** [-19.28]	-0.287*** [-19.20]
log($Overall\ TF_{ij}$)	-0.464*** [-13.64]				-0.247*** [-13.64]			
log($Overall\ TF_{i}$)			-0.222*** [-10.32]				-0.175*** [-10.32]	
log($Overall\ TF_{j}$)			-0.234*** [-10.33]				-0.193*** [-10.33]	
log($General\ TF_{ij}$)		-0.298*** [-8.203]				-0.147*** [-8.203]		
log($General\ TF_{i}$)				-0.106*** [-4.614]				-0.0796*** [-4.614]
log($General\ TF_{j}$)				-0.206*** [-7.322]				-0.149*** [-7.322]
log($Paperless\ TF_{ij}$)		-0.143*** [-6.647]				-0.118*** [-6.647]		
log($Paperless\ TF_{i}$)				-0.0941*** [-6.215]				-0.110*** [-6.215]
log($Paperless\ TF_{j}$)				-0.0462*** [-3.289]				-0.0603*** [-3.289]
R-squared	0.527	0.525	0.533	0.532	0.527	0.525	0.533	0.532
Adjusted R-squared	0.525	0.522	0.530	0.528	0.525	0.522	0.530	0.528

Notes: *** $p<0.01$, ** $p<0.05$, * $p<0.1$; t-stat. in square brackets; reporter and partner income group fixed effects were used in all models and are jointly statistically significant; 3,151 observations were used in all models

As noted previously, the overall TF implementation variable (*Overall TF$_{ij}$*)[11] used in Model (I.1) is the average of TF implementations rates of countries i and j. To isolate the impact of countries' own TF implementation from trade partners' TF implementation, Model (II.1) includes country's own overall implementation rate (*Overall TF$_i$*) as well as trade partner's implementation rate (*Overall TF$_j$*) as explanatory variables. The results show that approximately a 2% reduction of trade costs is expected when there is a 10% improvement in a country's own TF implementation and a further 2% reduction when trade partners improve their TF implementation by 10%. The latter finding is particularly important for developed countries since they already have high TF implementation rates, with little scope for TF implementation improvements to achieve further trade costs reductions. However, by cooperating on trade facilitation plurilaterally and multilaterally with trade partners, such as through the WTO TFA and the Framework Agreement on Facilitation of Cross-border Paperless Trade in Asia and the Pacific, significant gains in trade costs reduction can still be achieved by the developed countries.

Next, this study disaggregates the impact of overall trade facilitation (*Overall TF*), which is the combined effect of the WTO TFA and other TF measures. Models (I.2) and (II.2) replace Overall trade facilitation (*Overall TF*) variable with General implementation (combination of transparency, formalities, and institutional arrangements and cooperation measures under the WTO TFA, *General TF*), and Paperless and cross-border paperless TF implementation (other measures that go beyond the commitment under the WTO TFA, *Paperless TF*). Results suggest that implementation of general trade facilitation measures and paperless trade and cross-border paperless trade measures are both highly significant determinants of trade costs.

Model (I.2) shows a 10% improvement in general trade facilitation (*General TF$_{ij}$*) results in a 3.0% reduction in trade costs, while improvement in paperless and cross-border paperless TF measures implementation (*Paperless TF$_{ij}$*) by 10% is associated with a 1.4% reduction in trade costs. The effects of improvements of countries' own implementation and those of trading partners are mixed. Model (II.2) shows while a country's 10% own improvement of general trade facilitation (*General TF$_i$*) is associated with a 1.1% decline in trade costs, a similar improvement in a country's own paperless and cross-border paperless trade measures (*General TF$_i$*) results in a 0.9% reduction in trade costs. At the same time, a 10% improvement in trade partner's implementation of general trade facilitation measures (*General TF$_j$*) is associated with approximately a 2.1% reduction in trade costs, while an improvement by 10% in trade partner's paperless and cross-border paperless trade measures (*Paperless TF$_j$*) reduces trade costs by 0.5%.

The findings strongly support two important conclusions in implementing trade facilitation measures. First, general trade facilitation measures, which are often less complex and less costly to implement than other measures, can assist towards reducing trade costs. Once countries have reached the basic obligations associated with the WTO TFA, they should proactively adopt modern ICTs to trade procedures as well as implement electronic Single Window systems and other paperless trade measures. Second, there are synergic effects of trade facilitation implementation in reducing trade costs. Effects of trade costs reduction are from both own implementation as well as trade partners' implementation of trade facilitation measures. As such, by cooperating on trade facilitation plurilaterally and multilaterally with trade partners through agreements such as the Framework Agreement on Facilitation of Cross-border Paperless Trade in Asia and the Pacific, significant gains in trade costs reduction can still be achieved by the developed countries, who already have high levels of trade facilitation implementation.

The scope for making a 10% improvement varies significantly across factors and it is therefore useful in calculating standardized coefficients, which take into account the underlying data distribution of explanatory factors across the sample of countries considered. As shown in figure 2.3a, doing this highlights the importance of maritime connectivity as a dominant factor of trade cost variations across countries. It also confirms the importance of trade facilitation implementation in reducing trade costs. However, it also reveals that trade costs are not very sensitive to tariff reductions – essentially because tariffs have already been reduced drastically over the past two decades. It also confirms that distance and landlockedness remain key natural barriers to international trade. Examining trade facilitation implementation into details (see figure 2.3b), leading factors are those of general trade facilitation category. However, there is a mixed result on magnitudes of impact in trade costs reductions from the category of trade facilitation when considering the effects from own country and trading partner improvements.

---

[11]   WTO TFA measures and other selected trade facilitation measures beyond the WTO TFA

Figure 2.3. Sensitivity of trade costs to natural and policy factors

2.3a. Sensitivity of trade costs to natural and policy factors (combined effect)

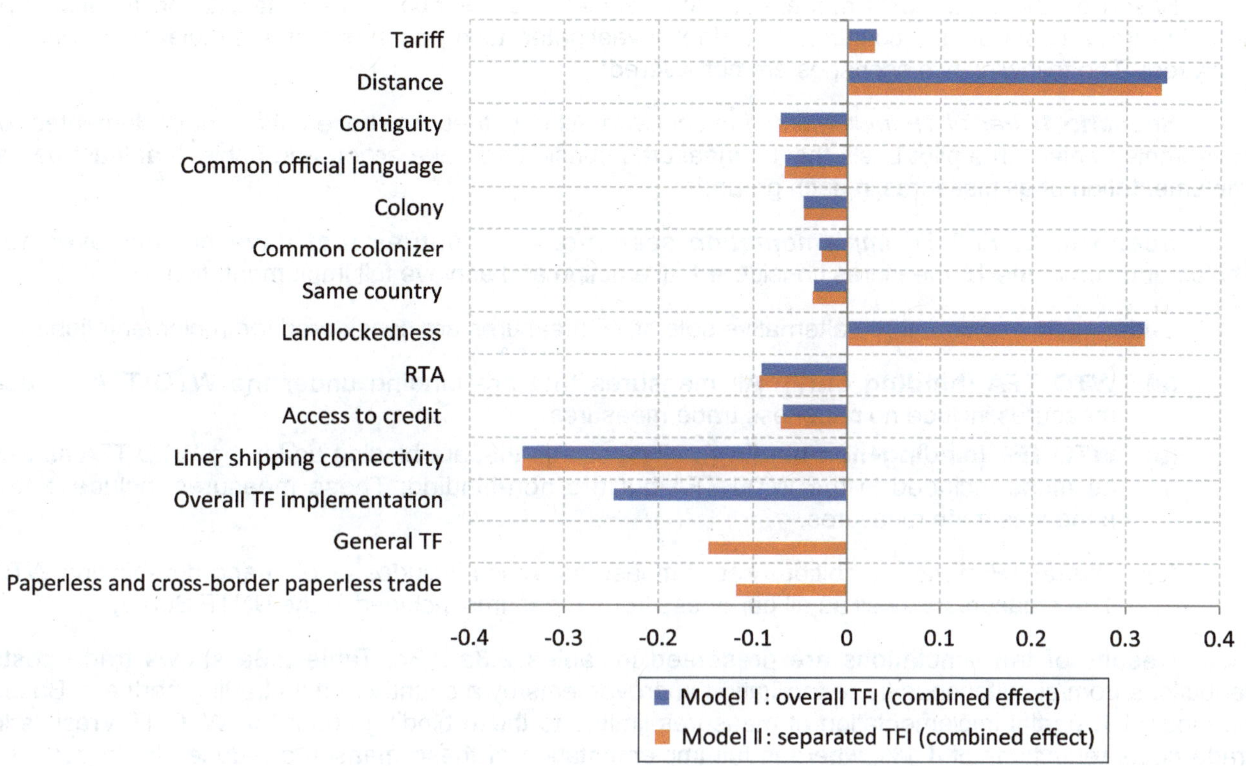

2.3b. Sensitivity of trade costs to trade facilitation implementation

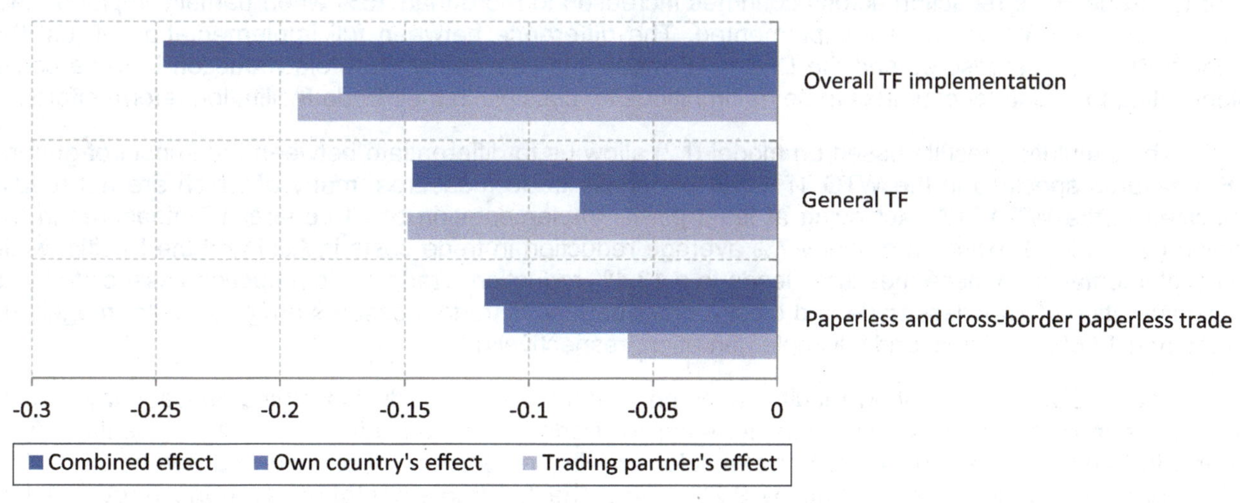

Source: Authors' own calculations.
Note: The figure shows standardized regression coefficients of all models in this study.

2.4. Impact of trade facilitation implementation on trade costs in Asia-Pacific: A "what if" analysis

Based on the trade costs model estimated earlier, the potential of trade facilitation measures in reducing trade costs across countries is further investigated using counterfactual simulations ("what if" analyses). The following two scenarios are considered:

Scenario 1: *Partial TF implementation scenario:* All countries that have either not implemented, or have implemented on a pilot basis the TF measures considered, take action and achieve at least partial implementation of all measures in each group;[12]

Scenario 2: *Full TF implementation scenario*: All countries that have not achieved full implementation of the TF measures considered take action and achieve full implementation.

Under each scenario, three alternative sets of TF measures are considered for implementation:

(a) **WTO TFA (binding only):** All measures that are binding under the WTO TFA; These measures include no paperless trade measures.

(b) **WTO TFA (binding+non-binding):** all measures that are binding under the WTO TFA as well as those included in the WTO TFA but are non-binding; These measures include a few paperless trade measures.

(c) **Digital TF:** a more ambitious set of measures, which includes binding and non-binding WTO TFA measures as well as all paperless trade measures included in the UNTF Survey.

Results of the simulations are presented in tables 2.3a-2.3c. Table 2.3a shows trade costs reductions from simultaneous trade facilitation improvements by a country and its trading partners. Based on model I.1, partial implementation of measures limited to those binding under the WTO TFA results in trade costs reductions of 4.1%, whereas full implementation of these measures reduces trade costs by 9.0%. In contrast, implementation of binding and non-binding WTO TFA measures results in a reduction of 7.2% in trade costs under a partial implementation scenario, and a 15% reduction under the more ambitious full implementation scenario. When the Digital TF set of measures are implemented, the average trade costs reduction across countries increases to more than 16% when partially implemented, and more than 26% when fully implemented. The difference between full implementation of just the binding WTO TFA measures and the Digital TF measures is a nearly threefold reduction in trade costs, highlighting the need for countries to be as ambitious as possible in their trade facilitation reform efforts.

The simulation results based on model (I.2) allow us to differentiate between the impact of general TF measures specified in the WTO TFA and paperless trade measures, many of which are not readily specified in the WTO TFA. Achieving at least partial implementation of all general TF measures in the region (scenario 1) results in a nearly 7% average reduction in trade costs in Asia and the Pacific, while full implementation of these measures leads to a 13.4% reduction. Trade costs reductions associated with implementation of paperless trade and cross-border paperless trade measures are of a similar magnitude (8.8% and 12.5% for partial and full implementation, respectively).

Tables 2.3b and 2.3c show results based on model II.1 and II.2, distinguishing between trade costs reductions from a country's own implementation of trade facilitation reform and those resulting from reform in trading partner countries. For example, own implementation of binding and non-binding WTO TFA measures reduces trade costs by 9.2% under the full implementation scenario (model II.1 in table 2.3b), while implementation of these measures by trade partners reduces trade costs of that country by up to 6.2% (model II.1 in table 2.3c). Similar results are obtained in the case of the Digital TF implementation, where own implementation reduces trade costs by 15.9% (model II.1 in table 2.3b), while implementation by trade partners reduces trade costs by 11.8% (model II.1 in table 2.3c).

---

[12] We follow the definition of "Partial implementation" and "Full implementation" in the UNTF Survey, also provided in Annex of Chapter 1 of this publication.

Table 2.3. Changes in international trade costs of Asia-Pacific as a result of trade facilitation improvements*

Table 2.3a Trade costs changes from trade facilitation in

Trade costs reduction from TFI improvement: Asia-Pacific	WTO TFA (binding)		WTO TFA (binding + non-binding)		Digital TF (binding + non-binding WTO TFA + other paperless and cross-border paperless)	
	Partially implemented	Fully implemented	Partially implemented	Fully implemented	Partially implemented	Fully implemented
Model I.1						
Overall TF	-4.07%	-8.98%	-7.20%	-14.98%	-16.47%	-26.17%
Model I.2						
General TF measures	-3.84%	-8.38%	-5.61%	-12.22%	-6.67%	-13.40%
Paperless and cross-border paperless trade	–	–	-1.65%	-2.78%	-8.81%	-12.47%

2.3b. Change on own country's trade facilitation implementation

Trade costs reduction from improvement on reporter side	WTO TFA (binding)		WTO TFA (binding + non-binding)		Digital TF (binding + non-binding WTO TFA + other paperless and cross-border paperless)	
	Partially implemented	Fully implemented	Partially implemented	Fully implemented	Partially implemented	Fully implemented
Model II.1						
Overall TF	-2.65%	-5.60%	-4.51%	-9.16%	-10.05%	-15.91%
Model II.2						
General TF measures	-1.77%	-3.69%	-2.46%	-5.28%	-2.92%	-5.80%
Paperless and cross-border paperless trade	–	–	-1.43%	-2.32%	-6.98%	-9.65%

2.3c. Change on trading partners' trade facilitation implementation

Trade costs reduction from improvement on partner side	WTO TFA (binding)		WTO TFA (binding + non-binding)		Digital TF (binding + non-binding WTO TFA + other paperless and cross-border paperless)	
	Partially implemented	Fully implemented	Partially implemented	Fully implemented	Partially implemented	Fully implemented
Model II.1						
Overall TF	-1.41%	-3.48%	-2.72%	-6.20%	-6.90%	-11.83%
Model II.2						
General TF measures	-1.94%	-4.68%	-3.07%	-7.17%	-3.70%	-7.90%
Paperless and cross-border paperless trade	–	–	-0.37%	-0.67%	-2.38%	-3.56%

Source: Authors' calculations.
Note: * See Annex 2 of Duval et al. (2018) for full individual country results.

These results show that, while reduction in trade costs will come essentially from own implementation, significant additional trade costs reductions may be achieved by encouraging trade partners to implement trade facilitation measures. The results provide a good rationale for the strong support of developed economies and other countries with very high trade facilitation implementation rates for the WTO TFA, which encourages developing economies in accelerating trade facilitation reforms. It further shows that leading trade facilitating economies have a strong incentive to support regional and multilateral cooperation on trade facilitation. This is particularly true in the case of cross-border paperless trade, which cannot be achieved without simultaneous implementation in own and partner countries.

At the individual country level, trade cost reductions associated with the various scenarios vary from zero to more than 40% (see figures 2.4a for partial implementation and 2.4b for full implementation). The overall effects largely depend on each country's existing level of trade facilitation implementation. As figure 2.4b shows, most of the least developed countries and landlocked developing countries in Asia and the Pacific can expect trade cost reductions of 5% (in the case of the Lao People's Democratic Republic) to 24% (in the case of Afghanistan) from full simultaneous implementation of the WTO TFA binding measures alone. Trade costs reductions in most least developed countries and landlocked developing countries increase further to between 11% (the Lao People's Democratic Republic) and 32% (Afghanistan) with full implementation of binding and non-binding WTO TFA commitments. Achieving full digital trade facilitation in turn generates trade costs reductions of more than 22% in most least developed countries and landlocked developing countries.

Figure 2.4. Trade cost reductions from simultaneous improvements in trade facilitation in Asia-Pacific

2.4a. Partial implementation scenario

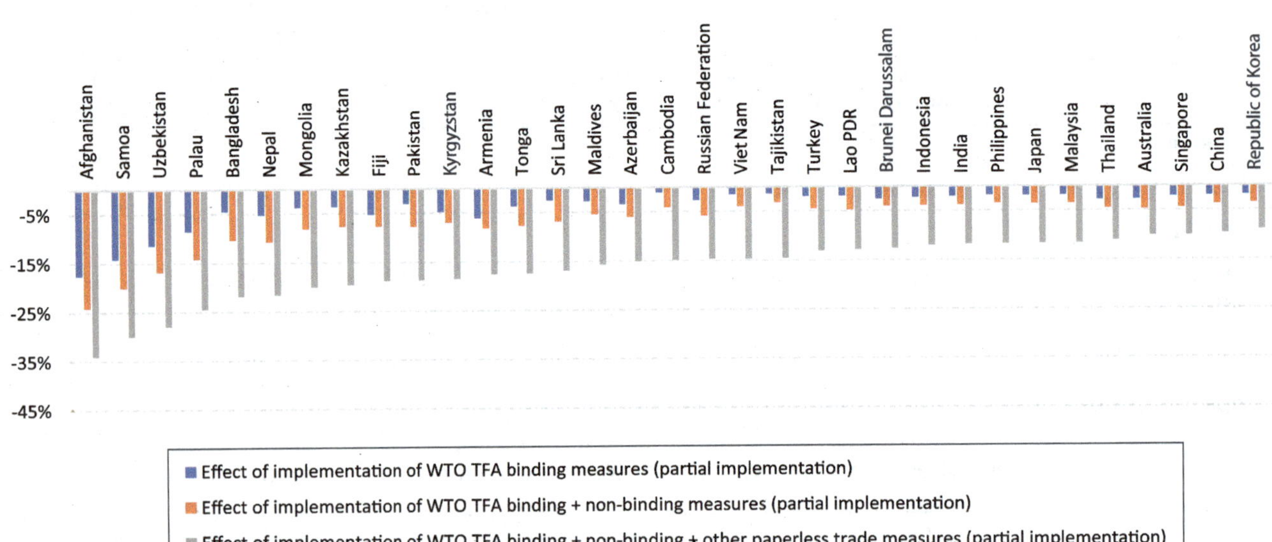

2.4b. Full implementation scenario

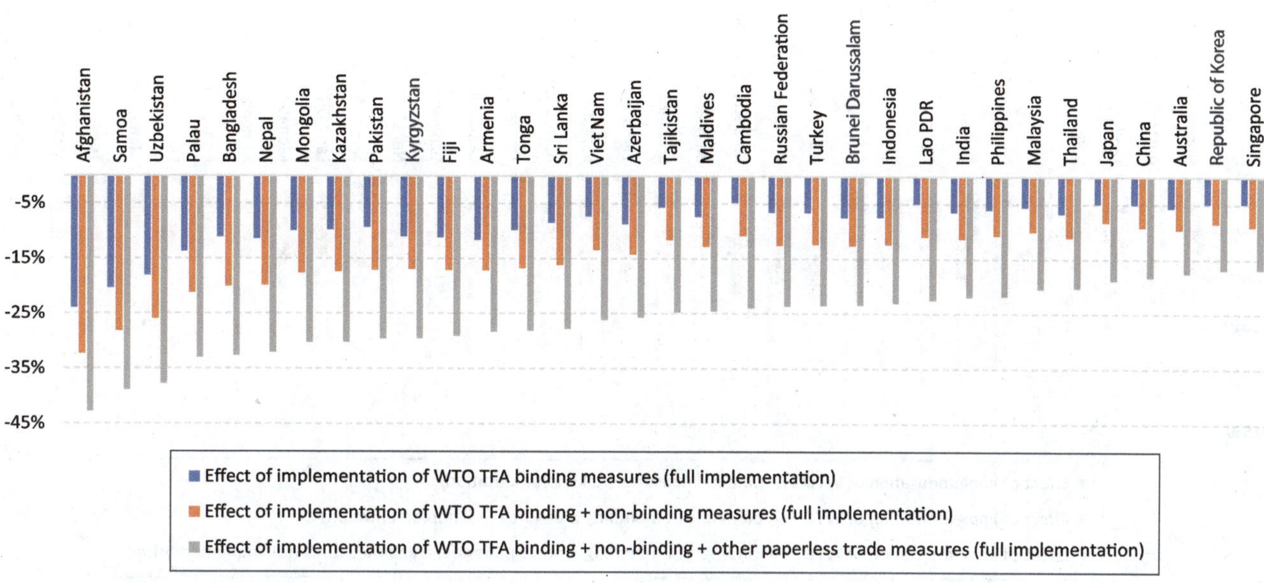

Source: Authors' calculations.

As emphasized earlier, economies with high rates of TF implementation can significantly benefit from trade partners' implementation. For example, ASEAN countries, such as Malaysia, Singapore and Thailand, and East Asian countries, such as China, Japan and Republic of Korea, whose implementation of the WTO TFA is already in place still benefit from trading partners' improvement in WTO TFA implementation (see figures 2.5a and 2.5b). Trade costs reductions as a result of trading partners' improvement under the WTO TFA+ Digital TF scenario ranges from 8% to 9% under partial implementation scenario and from 13% to 15% under full implementation scenario. Such cost reductions are significant and important in terms of improving the overall efficiency of the multilateral trading system, contributing to making it more inclusive and sustainable and facilitating development of global production networks. However, they should be clearly differentiated from trade cost reductions achieved through self-implementation of trade facilitation reform since they do not inherently affect a country's relative trade competitiveness.

Figure 2.5. Trade cost reductions from trading partners' improvements in trade facilitation in Asia-Pacific

2.5a. Partial implementation scenario

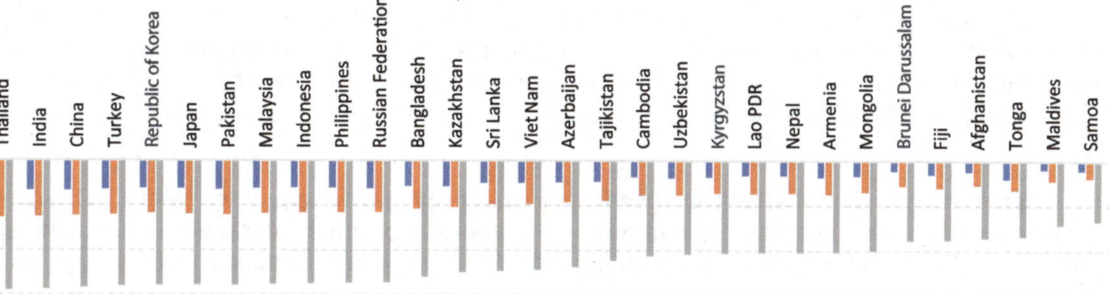

2.5b. Full implementation scenario

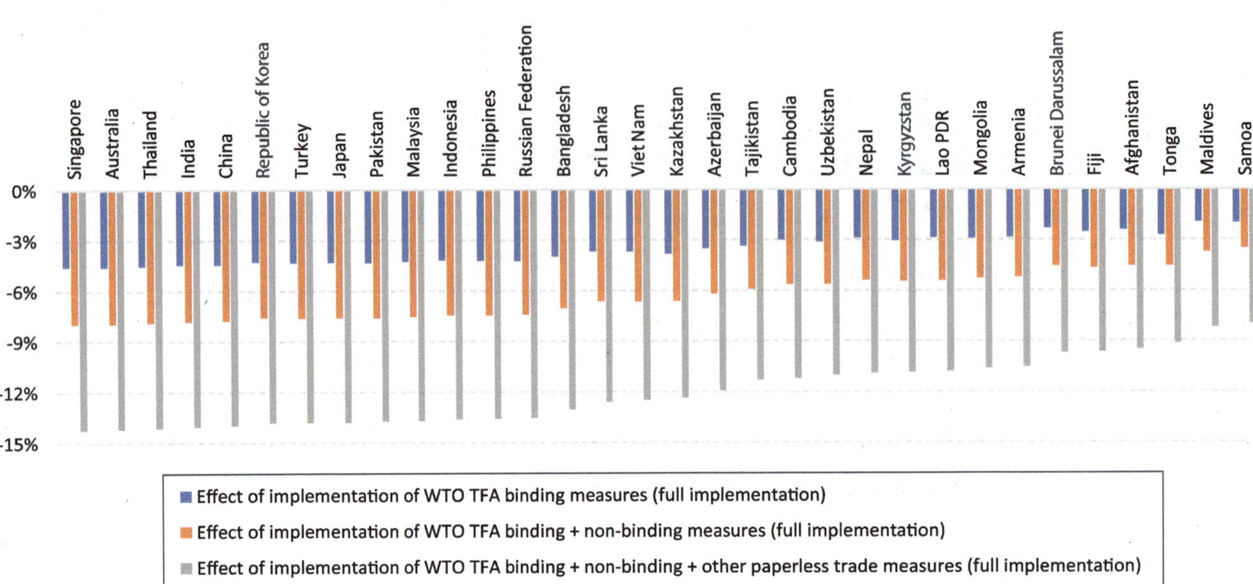

Source: Authors' calculations.

While the trade costs reductions from trade facilitation reform in general, and digital trade facilitation reform in particular, are impressive, it is worth emphasizing that it may be difficult to achieve full implementation in the short to medium term. Furthermore, several least developed countries and landlocked developing countries including, for example, Uzbekistan, Palau, Azerbaijan, are not WTO members. As such, these countries may not have access to the technical assistance committed by development partners under the WTO TFA.

At the same time, an interesting finding from the counterfactual simulations of trade facilitation implementation on trade costs is that many developing economies in Asia and the Pacific can expect only limited trade cost reductions from their own WTO TFA implementation, essentially because they have already implemented most of the measures featured in the agreement. This is particularly true for ASEAN and East Asian economies, where implementation of some of the most advanced measures featured in the WTO TFA – such as Single Windows – had been initiated well before the WTO TFA was concluded. Regional and multilateral initiatives and technical assistance that encourage less advanced countries to implement trade facilitation measures will provide more opportunities for the more advanced countries to further reduce trade costs. However, for these countries, making significant progress in reducing trade costs through trade facilitation necessarily implies focusing on digital trade facilitation and cross-border paperless trade measures.

To put these results into perspective, it is useful to contrast them with the trade costs reductions that may be associated with broader trade facilitation reforms, which often encompass measures aimed at improving trade-related infrastructure and services, and the overall business environment. In that context, the following additional counterfactual simulations were carried as part of this study using the results of model I.1 in table 2.2:

Scenario 3: *Improvement in maritime connectivity*: (a) all countries with LSCI scores below the developing countries' average improve their LSCI scores up to the average of developing countries, and (b) countries with the LSCI scores below the OECD average bring up their LSCI scores up to the OECD average;

Scenario 4: *Improvement in access to financing*: (a) all countries with CII scores below the developing countries' average improve their CII scores up to the average of developing countries, and (b) countries with the CII scores below the OECD average bring their CII scores up to the OECD average.

As shown in table 2.4, the results suggest that improvement in maritime connectivity, as described in Scenario 3, would reduce trade costs in Asia and the Pacific by approximately 8% to 9%. Improved access to finance through improvement in credit information availability and quality (Scenario 4) could

Table 2.4. Changes in trade costs of Asia-Pacific as a result of port connectivity and trade finance improvement

	LSCI improvement up to		Credit Index improvement up to	
	Developing countries' average	OECD average	Developing countries' average	OECD average
Simultaneous improvement	-8% / -9%	-13% / -14%	0% / -1%	-1% / -2%
Own improvement	4% / -6%	-6% / -8%	0% / -1%	0% / -2%
Trade partner improvement	-3% / -5%	-6% / -8%	0% / -1%	0% / -1%

Source: Authors' calculation.

Note: Counterfactual estimates based on models I and II, assuming port connectivity and credit information levels are brought up to the developing economies average and the OECD average.

reduce trade costs by at best 1%. As expected, the effect on trade costs reduction is greater when the improvement is pushed up to the OECD averages. Effects from countries' own improvement are similar in magnitude to the spillover effects from trading partners' improvement in maritime connectivity and access to trade finance.

Taken together, the size of the trade costs reductions associated with these broader trade facilitation measures appears to be significant, although they cannot be readily compared to those associated with implementation of the WTO TFA and paperless and cross-border paperless trade measures. It is noteworthy, however, that infrastructure improvement, as implied by improvements in LSCI scores, hold less promise to reduce trade costs than the arguably significantly less costly options of implementing WTO TFA and digital TF measures.

2.5. Conclusion

Using the data from the UNTF Survey, together with the latest available data from the World Bank-ESCAP Trade Cost Database, this chapter investigated the impact of implementing trade facilitation measures on trade costs. Impact of different sets of measures were considered, from a basic set of measures to ensure compliance with the WTO TFA commitment to a full set of digital trade facilitation measures. The study also disaggregated the effects of countries' own TF implementation from their trade partners' implementation. Important results may be summarized as follows.

First, full implementation of binding and non-binding measures included in the WTO TFA is associated with an average 15% trade cost reduction in Asia-Pacific, while implementation of binding measures only result in 9% trade costs reduction. This result clearly highlights the need for countries to fully implement the WTO TFA to reap significant benefits.

Second, implementation of digital trade facilitation can generate very significant trade costs reductions for most economies, reaching up to 40% for the least advanced economies. The magnitude of trade costs reductions from implementation of paperless trade and cross-border paperless trade measure is similar to that of implementing measures in the WTO TFA. The estimated impact of a full implementation of digital TF is associated with a 26.2% decrease in international trade costs in the Asia and the Pacific region, or savings in international transaction costs of about $1.2 trillion. Overall, an ambitious digital trade facilitation strategy could nearly double the trade costs reductions expected from the WTO TFA compliance alone.

Third, the analysis confirmed that there are significant reductions in trade costs associated with trade partners' implementation of trade facilitation measures. This shows that economies which already have high rates of trade facilitation implementation have strong incentive to encourage and support their trading partners in implementing trade facilitation. Further facilitation of trade in these economies will involve developing legal and technical frameworks to support cross-border paperless trade, i.e., enabling the electronic exchange and legal recognition of trade data and documents between public and private actors located in different countries along the international supply chain, as envisaged in the recently adopted Framework Agreement on Facilitation of Cross-Border Paperless Trade in Asia and the Pacific. At the national level, such efforts should best take place within the context of broader trade facilitation programmes and strategies encompassing trade-related infrastructure and services, particularly those related to maritime connectivity and access to finance.

References

ADB and ESCAP (2017). Trade Facilitation and Better Connectivity for an Inclusive Asia and Pacific. Available at http://www.adb.org/sites/default/files/publication/359786/trade-facilitation-connectivity.pdf

Arvis, J.F., Duval, Y., Shepherd, B., and Utoktham, C. (2013). Trade Costs in the Developing World: 1995-2010. World Bank Policy Research Working Paper No. 6309.

Duval, Y., Wang, T., Malakoudi, D., and Bayona, P. (2015). Trade Facilitation Implementation in Asia-Pacific 2015: Moving Towards Paperless Trade. United Nations ESCAP Trade Insights, Issue No.12.

Duval, Y., Utoktham, C., and Kravchenko, A. (2018). Impact of implementation of digital trade facilitation on trade cost, ARTNeT Working Paper Series, No. 174 January 2018, Bangkok, ESCAP.

ESCAP (2015). Reducing Trade Costs in Asia-Pacific Developing Countries. Studies in Trade and Investment 84. United Nations ESCAP. Available at: http://www.unescap.org/publications/reducing-trade-costs-asia-pacific-developing-countries-studies-trade-and-investment-no

Novy, D. (2013). Gravity Redux: Measuring International Trade Costs with Panel Data. Economic Inquiry, 51(1), 101-121.

OECD (2015). Implementation of the WTO Trade Facilitation Agreement: The Potential Impact on Trade Costs. The OECD Website, Trade and Agriculture Directorate. Available at http://www.oecd.org/trade/tradedev/WTO-TF-Implementation-Policy-Brief_EN_2015_06.pdf

Wang, T., Duval, Y., and Malakoudi, D.T. (2015). Joint United Nations Regional Commissions Trade Facilitation and Paperless Trade Implementation Survey 2015 Asia and the Pacific Report. United Nations ESCAP. Available at: http://unnext.unescap.org/UNTFsurvey2015.asp

WTO (2015). World Trade Report 2015: Speeding up trade: benefits and challenges of implementing the WTO Trade Facilitation Agreement. Available at https://www.wto.org/english/res_e/booksp_e/world_trade_report15_e.pdf

Chapter 3

Digital trade facilitation in regional trade agreements

3.1. Introduction

As part of their continuous efforts to harness international trade for sustainable development, Asia-Pacific economies have long strived to make trade procedures as efficient as possible, in particular through implementation of automated customs systems, electronic single windows and other digital trade facilitation initiatives. These paperless trade measures are rapidly becoming essential not only to maintain trade competitiveness, but also to address the trade control and logistics challenges associated with an increase in small shipments and cross-border e-commerce.[1]

Paperless trade generally refers to the conduct of international trade transactions using electronic rather than paper-based data and documents.[2] It is more formally defined as trade "taking place on the basis of electronic communications, including exchange of trade-related data and documents in electronic form" in the Framework Agreement on Facilitation of Cross-border Paperless Trade in Asia and the Pacific (FA-PT) adopted by the member States of United Nations Economic and Social Commission for Asia and the Pacific (ESCAP) in May 2016.[3] While the ultimate goal of paperless trade is to dematerialize all information flows associated with a given transaction for all stakeholders, paperless trade initiatives generally focus on facilitating data and documents flows between businesses and government (BtoG) and/or between to governments (GtoG).[4]

Paperless trade generates significant economy-wide savings, including direct savings to traders in the form of lower compliance costs, as well as indirect savings from faster movement of goods and lower inventory costs.[5] It also enhances opportunities for small and medium enterprises (SMEs) to participate in cross-border trade, affords timely availability of shipping documents and reduces errors associated with re-keying of data.[6] In addition, through reduction in clearance times, it can increase port efficiency and reduce port congestion and related problems.[7] Potential annual export gains associated with moving from manual paper-based trade to paperless trade have been estimated at between \$36 billion and \$257 billion in Asia-Pacific, depending on the extent of automation and dematerialization of procedures and documents.[8]

---

[1]   UNCTAD (2015), among others, indicate that cross-border e-commerce has led to a 48% growth in the volume of international deliveries of small packets between 2011 and 2014. The etradeforall.org initiative identifies trade logistics and facilitation as one of seven key areas for e-trade development.

[2]   Sung Heun Ha and Sang Won Lim (2014). See also ECE and WEF (2017).

[3]   This new United Nations treaty, dedicated to enabling paperless trade among Asia and the Pacific member States opened for signature and ratification or accession in New York on 1 October 2016. See: http://www.unescap.org/resources/framework-agreement-facilitation-cross-border-paperless-trade-asia-and-pacific

[4]   This is in contrast to e-commerce, where the focus is generally on facilitating exchange of information between business and consumers (BtoC) and/or between to businesses (BtoB). In the international trade context, paperless trade is seen as an enabler of cross-border e-commerce, with general provisions on "paperless trade" or "paperless trading" increasingly included in e-commerce chapters of regional trade or economic partnership agreements (e.g., in the TPP).

[5]   See for example, UNNExT Briefs on single window implementation in Republic of Korea, as well as Senegal, Singapore and Thailand. http://unnext.unescap.org

[6]   See for example, Laryea (2005).

[7]   See Laryea (2002).

[8]   Shepherd and Duval (2015). This is made possible by the very significant time and cost savings associated with the digitalization of the entire trade process, with direct cost savings alone estimated at USD 7 billion annually in Asia and the Pacific – and time savings in the export process of at least 24%.

Importantly, the use of electronic rather than paper documents can also help enhance regulatory control and compliance by governments, especially when relevant data and documents can be exchanged among agencies and across borders. In particular, the availability or more accurate and timely data in electronic form can enable trade control agencies to more efficiently evaluate the compliance risks associated with individual shipments, enabling them to identify high-risk transactions, ultimately boosting Customs revenue while also speeding up the trade of compliant traders.[9]

Overall, the significant benefits for both governments and traders have led an increasing number of countries to promote paperless trade, including as part of multilateral and regional trade agreements. Accordingly, this paper analyses the extent to which recent regional trade agreements have included provisions related to paperless trade globally, using the World Trade Organization Trade Facilitation Agreement (WTO TFA) as a reference. The results provide insights and models for future negotiations in this area, as well as for implementation of the FA-PT.

Our analysis reveals that more than half of the trade agreements which have entered into force since 2005 globally (90 of 138) include paperless trade measures or provisions. Thirty of these regional trade agreements (RTAs) reviewed in this study contain a dedicated provision titled "Paperless Trading" or "Paperless Trade Administration", typically found either in the Chapter on e-commerce, or the one dealing with Customs procedures and trade facilitation. As shown in figure 1, the detailed analysis presented in this paper reveals that the number of paperless trade measures included in RTAs almost doubled between 2005-2008 and 2013-2016. While the impact of including such measures and provisions in trade agreements is difficult to measure, the willingness of governments to systematically include commitments in this area is a welcome development.

Figure 3.1. Number of Paperless Trade Measures in RTAs (2005-2016)

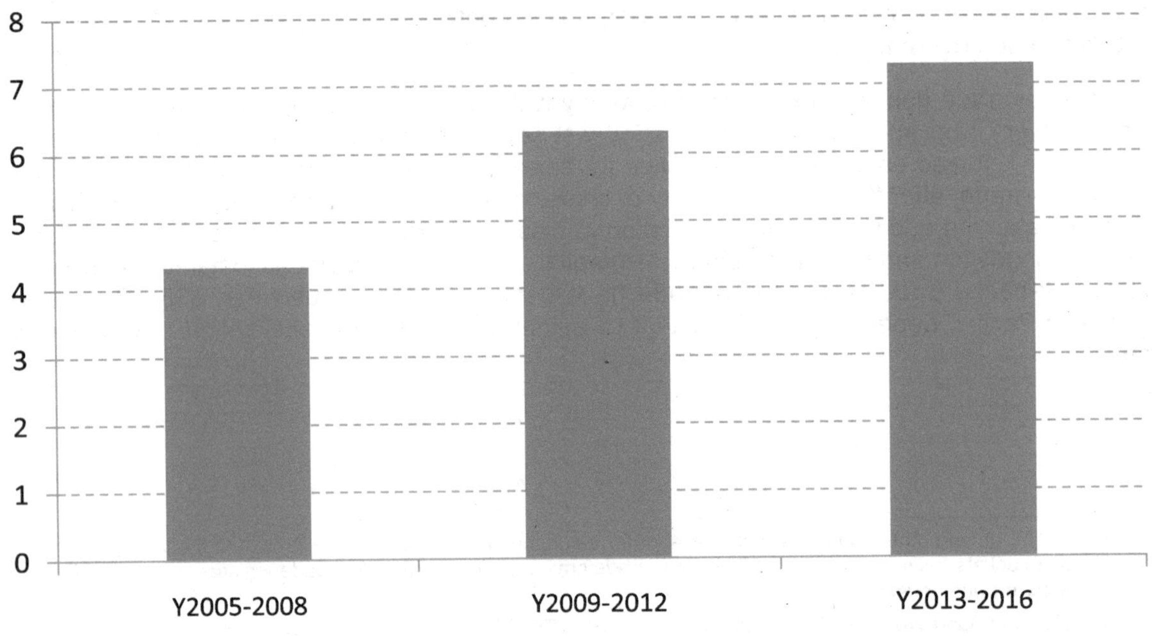

Source: ESCAP calculations.

---

[9] For example, Ghana Customs reports that its electronic Single Window launched in 2015 helped boost revenue collection by almost 15% in one year, while cutting down waiting time and approval for classification of goods from 2 weeks to 2 days – See more at: http://thebftonline.com/business/economy/21250/single-window-boosts-revenue-collection-148-in-one-year.html#sthash.bASAWHGE.dpuf

The chapter is organized as follows: the next section presents a typology of paperless trade measures and provisions in RTAs, providing a basis for the evaluation of the paperless trade coverage of such agreements. The results of the evaluation are then presented, highlighting differences in coverage by geographic regions and identifying the least and most common measures included in RTAs. This is followed by a more detailed analysis of selected RTAs in the Asia-Pacific region, including a comparative analysis of "Paperless Trading"/"Paperless Trade Administration" Articles and an assessment of relevant paperless trade measures in terms of substance and nature (binding vs. best endeavour). Linkages to provisions featured in the new FA-PT are then discussed, followed by conclusions.

3.2. Typology of paperless trade related provisions

An initial starting point for the development of a list of paperless trade measures and provisions is the United Nations Global Survey on Trade Facilitation and Paperless Trade Implementation (UNTF Survey.[10]) The paperless trade and cross-border paperless trade measures included in the 2015 UNTF Survey are shown in table 3.1.

Paperless trade measures featured in the UNTF Survey include the establishment of electronic automated customs system and electronic single window system, electronic submission of trade-related documents including trade licenses, sea/air cargo manifests and customs declarations, and electronic application and issuance of trade licenses and preferential certificate of origin. Furthermore, there are six measures related to cross-border paperless trade in the survey. Apart from the general measure "Engagement of the country in trade-related cross-border electronic data exchange with other countries", the measures aiming at exchanging specific documents such as Sanitary and Phytosanitary (SPS) Certificates and Certificates of Origin (COO) electronically are included. In addition, two of the measures,

Table 3.1. Paperless Trade Measures included in the 2015 Global Survey on Trade Facilitation and Paperless Trade Implementation

Paperless trade	15. Electronic/Automated Customs System established (e.g., ASYCUDA)
	16. Internet connection available to Customs and other trade control agencies at border-crossings
	17. Electronic Single Window System
	18. Electronic submission of Customs declarations
	19. Electronic Application and Issuance of Trade Licenses
	20. Electronic Submission of Sea Cargo Manifests
	21. Electronic Submission of Air Cargo Manifests
	22. Electronic Application and Issuance of Preferential Certificate of Origin
	23. E-Payment of Customs Duties and Fees
	24. Electronic Application for Customs Refunds
Cross-border paperless trade	25. Laws and regulations for electronic transactions are in place (e.g. e-commerce law, e-transaction law)
	26. Recognized certification authority issuing digital certificates to traders to conduct electronic transactions
	27. Engagement of the country in trade-related cross-border electronic data exchange with other countries
	28. Certificate of Origin electronically exchanged between your country and other countries
	29. Sanitary and Phytosanitary Certificate electronically exchanged between your country and other countries
	30. Banks and insurers in your country retrieving letters of credit electronically without lodging paper-based documents

Source: United Nations Global Survey on Trade Facilitation and Paperless Trade Implementation 2015.

---

[10]   UNNExT (2015). Global Survey on Trade Facilitation and Paperless Trade Implementation 2015. Available at: https://unnext.unescap.org/content/global-survey-trade-facilitation-and-paperless-trade-implementation-2015

"Laws and regulations for electronic transactions" and "Recognized certification authority issuing digital certificates to traders to conduct electronic transactions" are basic building blocks towards enabling the exchange and mutual recognition of trade-related data and documents among stakeholders within a country and also along the entire international supply chain.[11]

Following an initial review of regional trade agreements, however, most of the measures listed in the UNTF Survey were not frequently found in RTA provisions, probably because such measures were too "applied" and specific to be included in such – generally quite broad – legal instruments. We therefore further developed the list of paperless trade measures and provisions based on an iterative review of the text of agreements included in the WTO Regional Trade Agreements Information System (RTA-IS).

Our analysis covered all 136 RTAs included in the WTO RTA-IS database which had entered into force since the year 2005 and were available in the English language – as of September 2016.[12] The Trans-Pacific Partnership Agreement (TPP), as well as relevant intra-ASEAN agreements (i.e., the following three inter-related ASEAN agreements was reviewed together: ASEAN Trade in Goods Agreement, Agreement to Establish and Implement the ASEAN Single Window, ASEAN Agreement on Customs) were also considered and included in the analysis. The WTO Trade Facilitation Agreement (TFA) was used as a benchmark in the analysis.[13]

In line with the UNTF Survey, we adopted a broad definition of paperless trade in identifying relevant measures and provisions, looking for mentions of related keywords, in particular "information and communication technologies", "internet", "electronic", "automation", and "paperless", in chapters of the agreements covering not only trade facilitation and customs procedures but also those covering rules of origin, technical barriers to trade, sanitary and phytosanitary measures, financial services, as well as electronic commerce. However, the scope of paperless trade was not extended to chapters or sections related to transport and logistics services liberalization, mobility of business people, government procurement and intellectual property.

A typology of 27 paperless trade measures and provisions was ultimately developed, as shown in table 3.2.[14] While some of the measures and provisions included are relatively general (e.g. "E-submission/processing of trade-related data/documents"), we also included much more specific and sometimes overlapping measures and provisions in order to get a better understanding of the content and depth of the various agreements. Specific measures and provisions related to a more general measure included in table 2 are specified in italic immediately under such measure. We also try to distinguish between paperless trade measures and provisions focusing on exchange of information in electronic form between stakeholders domestically (measures and provisions No.1-14) from those more directly related to cross-border electronic data and document exchanges (measures No. 15-27). Finally, in line with the content of some of the most recent agreements and their e-commerce chapters, the typology emphasizes provisions related to e-certificates and e-signatures (16-21), focusing on their mutual recognition and interoperability in particular.[15]

---

[11] Ibid.

[12] The WTO RTA-IS included 156 RTAs which had entered into force on or after 2005, but RTAs whose texts are only available in Spanish and Russian were not reviewed.

[13] The complete list of the RTAs reviewed is available in Annex 1 of Yann Duval and Kong Menjing (2010). Digital trade Facilitation: Paperless trade in Regional Trade Agreements. Available from https://www.adb.org/publications/digital-trade-facilitation-paperless-trade-regional-trade-agreements

[14] See Monterio and Teh (2017) and Wu (2017) for alternative typologies developed as part of broader analysis of e-commerce provisions in RTAs.

[15] To make the list of paperless trade measures as comprehensive as possible, two specific measures included in the UNRCs Survey, namely E-submission of sea cargo manifest (no. 4) and E-application of customs refund (no. 10), are kept in the list although none of the trade agreements reviewed included them.

Table 3.2. Typology of Paperless Trade Measures and Provisions in PTAs

	Measure/Provision	Note
1	Acceptance of e-copies	This refers to accepting trade administration documents submitted electronically as the legal equivalent of the paper version of these documents. (e.g., Australia-Japan EPA Art. 13.9)
2	E-submission/processing of trade-related data/ documents	This includes the provision of advance lodging of electronic documents for pre-arrival processing, the electronic submission and processing of information necessary for the release of an express consignment before the express consignment arrives; and submission of a single document covering all goods imported in express consignment through electronic means. (e.g., Republic of Korea-New Zealand FTA Art. 4.4, 4.7, 4.8)
3	*E-submission of Sea Cargo Manifests*	Measure included in the UNTF Survey – and also covered by the WCO Revised Kyoto Convention and relevant International Maritime Organization (IMO) agreements
4	*E-submission of Air Cargo Manifests*	Refers to the submission of a manifest covering all goods contained in an express shipment through electronic means. (e.g., Republic of Korea-Viet Nam FTA Art. 4.7(c))
5	E-system of Export/Import Licenses or Permits	See, e.g., Treaty on the Eurasian Economic Union, Annex to the Protocol on Non-Tariff Regulatory Measures in Relation to Third Countries, Rules for Issuing Licenses and Permits for the Export and/or Import of Goods II.
6	E-system of SPS certificates	See, e.g., Trans-Pacific Partnership (TPP) Art. 7.12
7	E-system of COO	This includes COO e-certification system, the e-system for pre-export verification of the origin of the goods. In addition, making a claim for preferential tariff treatment by electronic means. (e.g., Australia-The PRC FTA Art. 3.16) and the issuance of CO in electronic format also implies the need for e-system of COO (e.g., India-Malaysia ECA Annex 3-3 7(a)). E-Systems for verification of COOs (e.g., The China-Chile FTA Annex 6) come under e-exchange of COOs.
8	E-record keeping	The documents to be maintained are related to exportation, importation, and may include copies of COO and other documentary evidence of origin. (e.g., The China-Singapore FTA Art. 31).
9	E-payment system	See, e.g., TPP Chapter 11 Section D.
10	E-application for customs refunds	Measure included in the TFPI Survey
11	E-Customs System/ Customs Automation	This measure includes electronic focal point, provided by customs administration, through which its traders may submit all required regulatory information in order to obtain clearance of goods (e.g., The PRC-Peru FTA Art. 54.4). In the agreement which mentions E-submission of customs declaration (e.g., EFTA-Colombia FTA Annex vii Art. 3.2(b))/forms (e.g., Canada-Colombia FTA Art. 413) implies customs automation. In addition, this measure includes the introduction of a single administrative document, or an electronic equivalent, for the purpose of establishing/filing customs declarations at the import and export stages (e.g., EU-Cameroon EPA Art. 35 1(b)) and the establishment of electronic means for all its customs reporting requirements (e.g., Australia-Chile Art. 5.11).
12	*Automated System for Risk Management and targeting*	This measure includes the provision of a single point for the documentary or electronic processing of those goods where a customs administration of a Party deems that the inspection of goods is not necessary to authorise clearance of the goods from customs control, which is mentioned in Article titled as "Risk management". (e.g., ASEAN-Australia-New Zealand FTA Chapter 4 Art. 9)
13	Single Window System	See, e.g., Agreement to Establish and Implement the ASEAN Single Window.

Table 3.2. *(continued)*

	Measure/Provision	**Note**
14	E-system for inter-organization communication	This measure includes electronic systems for information exchange between competent authorities and trading communities and electronic means for inter-agency communication. (Australia-The China FTA Art. 4.6). However, unlike Single Window System, single (one-time) submission of information by traders is not implied.
15	Laws for electronic transactions	The laws mentioned in this measure not only cover binding laws, regulations and measures made by competent authorities, but also includes self-regulations of private sectors. (e.g., Australia-Chile FTA Art. 16.5)
16	Use of electronic certificates and electronic signatures	This measure also covers e-signature or official seal of certificates of origin. (e.g., ASEAN-Australia-New Zealand FTA Chapter 10 Art. 5)
17	*(Mutual) determination of authentication technologies*	This measure includes Promoting the interoperability of infrastructure such as electronic authentication. (e.g., New Zealand-Taiwan Province of China PoC ECA Art. 9.2(c) (ii))
18	*Proving in court legal compliance of E-authentication*	See, e.g., ASEAN-Australia-New Zealand FTA Chapter 10 Art. 5.
19	*Meeting standards for E-signature and E-authentication*	See, e.g., Australia-Japan EPC Art. 13.6.
20	*Mutual recognition of digital certificates and E-signature*	See, e.g., ASEAN-Australia-New Zealand FTA Chapter 10 Art. 5.
21	*Interoperability of digital certificates used by business*	See, e.g., ASEAN-Australia-New Zealand FTA Chapter 10 Art. 5.
22	Trade-related electronic data exchange	This measure covers the development of electronic systems to facilitate government-to-government exchange of international trade data (e.g., CAFTA-DR Art. 5.3), the establishment and use of ICT for electronic data exchange. (e.g., Republic of Korea-Viet Nam FTA Art. 4.3(c))
23	*E-exchange of COO related information*	This includes the direct communications between the competent governmental authority of the exporting Party and the customs authority of the importing Party through email of such information (e.g., Japan-Thailand EPC, Operational Procedures referred to in Chapter 2 (Trade in Goods) and Chapter 3 (Rules of Origin) Rule 11). It also includes the development of electronic systems for checking the authenticity of a COO (e.g., The China-Chile FTA Annex 6).
24	*E-exchange of SPS related information*	Includes use of technological means of communication, such as electronic communication, video or telephone conference to discuss SPS related matters (e.g., Iceland-The China FTA Art. 19)
25	*E-exchange of TBT related information*	Includes exchange of TBT related information through electronic mail, teleconferencing, videoconferencing (e.g., Australia-Republic of Korea FTA Art. 5.10)
26	*E-transmission of financial information*	The information covers letters of credit, insurance certificates and etc. which are exchanged between financial institutions of parties for data-processing. (e.g., Canada-Republic of Korea FTA, Annex 10-B Section C)
27	Use of international standards for paperless trade	Refers to the use of international standards when implementing any of the above-mentioned measures

Source: Authors' calculations

3.3. Paperless trade coverage of RTAs

To provide an overall picture of the paperless trade coverage in recent RTAs, we review how many of the 27 measures identified above are included in each of the RTAs included in the study.[16] For each measure in table 3.2, an agreement gets a "1" if the measure is mentioned in any form or language, i.e., regardless of whether it is simply authorized or encouraged, or whether it is formulated as a binding or exclusive commitment – and a "0" otherwise. Ninety RTAs (66%) are found to contain at least one paperless trade measure.[17]

Figure 3.2. Paperless trade coverage in RTAs of East Asian Economies since 2005

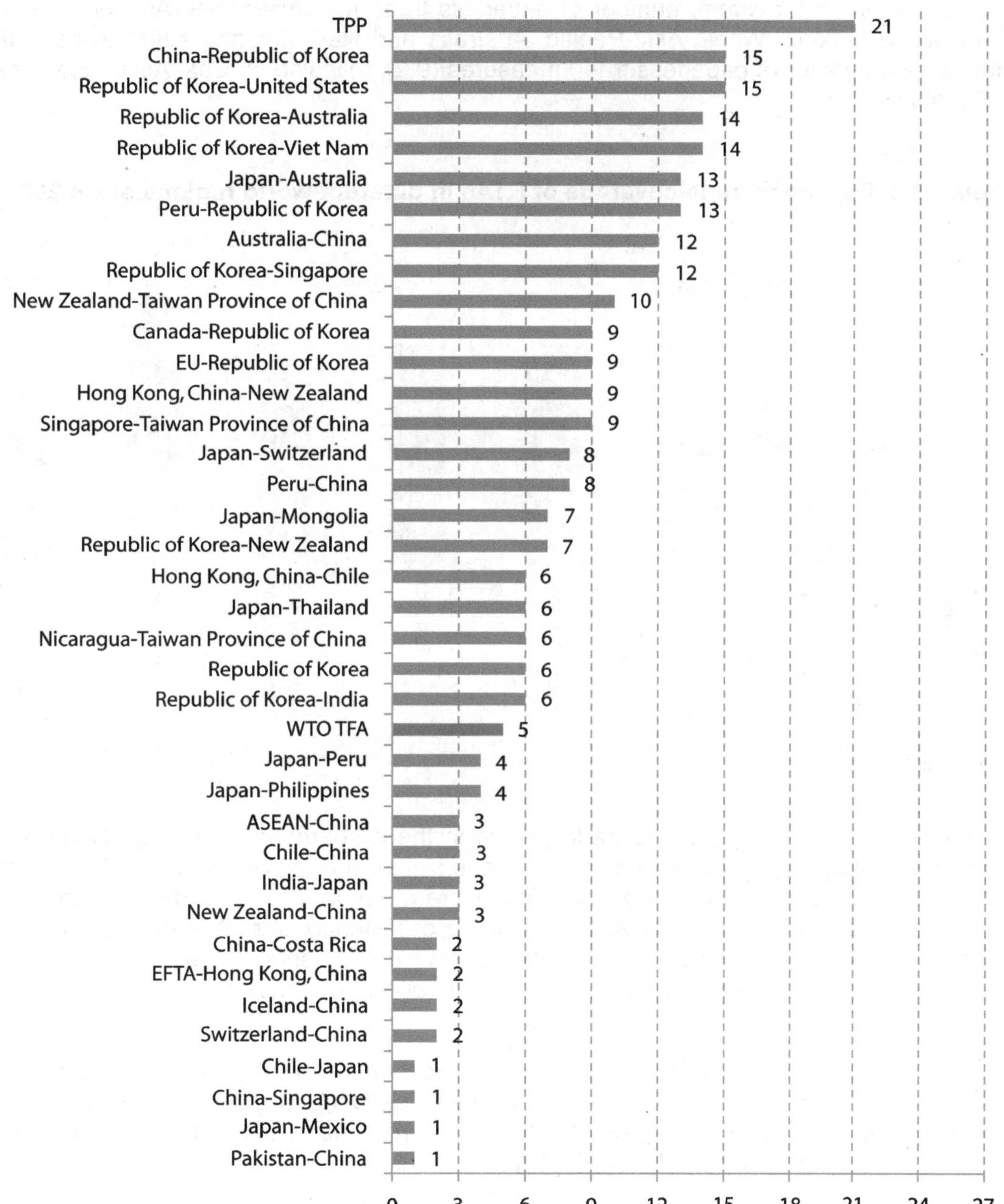

Source: Authors
Note: The figure shows the number of paperless trade measures mentioned in each agreement (out of 27).

---

[16] More information on the RTAs included is available in Annex 1.

[17] The same weight is given to all 27 measures, although arguments could be made that some measures are more important or far reaching than others. It is worth noting, however, that the same RTAs emerge as paperless trade "leaders" when only general measures are counted (i.e., the 12 sub measures shown in italic in table 3.2 are excluded from the analysis).

Figure 3.2 shows how many paperless trade measures are mentioned in each of the RTAs which are signed by East Asian economies. Among all agreements considered, the Trans-Pacific Partnership (TPP) Agreement has the highest number of paperless trade measures – its text refers to 21 of the 27 measures and provisions considered in our analysis. This Agreement is not only the largest but also the newest of the regional trade agreements considered in this study – and the only one that has not yet entered into force, providing further evidence of the growing interest in cross-border paperless trade. The second most comprehensive agreement on paperless trade is the Republic of Korea-United States Agreement ("KOR-US"), with 15 measures included, followed by the bilateral agreements between Republic of Korea and Viet Nam ("KOR-VN") featuring 14.[18] As a reference, the WTO TFA only features five measures and provisions on paperless trade.

Figure 3.3 shows the average number of paperless trade measures in RTAs signed by countries from different world regions. Within Asia-Pacific, Australia and New Zealand seem to have the RTAs featuring the largest number of paperless trade measures (9.2), followed by East Asian economies (7.1), led by the Republic of Korea.

Figure 3.3. Paperless trade coverage of RTAs in different world regions since 2005

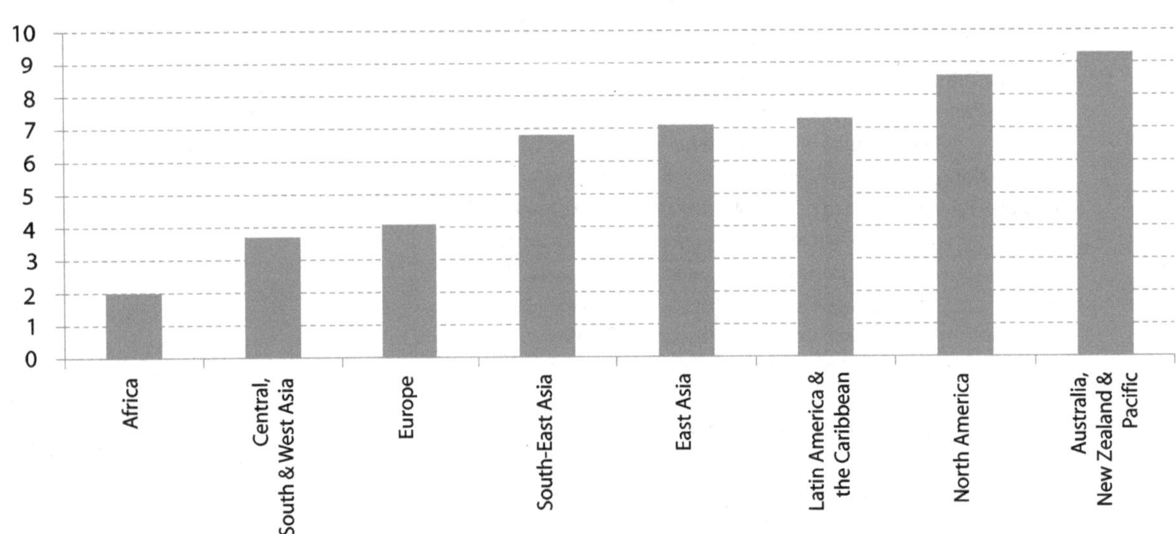

Source: Authors' calculations

The average number of paperless trade shown in the agreements signed by South-East Asian economies is 6.8. Singapore, as the economy which has signed the highest number of RTAs containing paperless trade measures, leads South-East Asia in this area.[18] In general, ASEAN plays an active role in including paperless trade measures in RTA rule-making. For instance, Intra-ASEAN agreements contain 10 paperless trade measures. But the content of its ASEAN+ agreements vary widely, from 12 measures featured in the ASEAN-Australia-New Zealand FTA to only one in the case, for example, of the ASEAN-India FTA.

The average number of paperless trade measures mentioned in RTAs signed by Central and South Asian as well as Middle-East economies is merely 4.[19] India leads that region with the highest number of RTAs involving paperless trade measures (5), three of which have the same or higher number of paperless trade measures than that in the WTO TFA.

---

[18] Many of the most comprehensive RTAs in terms of paperless trade are between Asia-Pacific Economic Cooperation (APEC) member economies. APEC, through its Electronic Commerce Steering Group and Paperless Trade Subgroup (ECSG), has actively promoted paperless trading among its members, in particular between 2002 and 2012. See, e.g., ECSG (2004).

[19] For details, see Annex 2 of Yann Duval and Kong Menjing (2010). Digital trade Facilitation: Paperless trade in Regional Trade Agreements. Available from https://www.adb.org/publications/digital-trade-facilitation-paperless-trade-regional-trade-agreements

Interestingly, while the European Union (EU) has strived to develop paperless trade systems among its members,[20] our analysis suggests that it has put limited emphasis on paperless trade in its RTAs, with an average number of paperless trade measures (4) barely on par with that of the WTO TFA. In contrast, many RTAs signed by North American economies, in particular the United States and Canada, feature 8 or more paperless trade measures. RTAs signed by Caribbean, Central American and South American Economies also feature a significant number of paperless trade measures, in part because many of these agreements involve the United States or other Asia-Pacific Economic Cooperation (APEC) member countries. Peru leads other developing American economies in this area, being both the country with the highest number of RTAs containing paperless trade measures and member of one of the most comprehensive RTA in this area (US-Peru FTA).[21]

3.3.1. Frequency of paperless trade measures in RTAs

The paperless trade content of RTAs appears to be relatively diverse, with no single measure included in our typology mentioned in more than half of the 90 RTAs featuring at least one paperless trade related measure or provision. As shown in figure 3.4, "The use of international standards for electronic exchange of data and documents" is most frequently mentioned in RTAs (47%), along with provisions on "Promoting e-certification and e-signatures" (47%) and the need for "Laws to enable electronic transactions" (44%). Other more frequently mentioned general measures in the RTAs include general provisions encouraging Electronic submission of trade-related data and documents, Electronic record keeping, and Acceptance of electronic copies.

Interestingly, several specific measures are also frequently mentioned. Measures related to Electronic exchange of information on technical barriers to trade (TBT) across borders are mentioned in more than 44% of the RTAs with at least one paperless trade measures,[22] while 38% of these RTAs mention electronic or automated customs systems (37%). Measures related to the "Electronic transmission of financial information across border between banks or private parties" are also found in more than 27% of the RTAs.

The notion of "Electronic systems to facilitate inter-agency communications and collaboration" is featured in some form in nearly 25% of the RTAs with at least one paperless trade measure. However, "Single Window" facilities, which are the subject of a dedicated provision in the WTO TFA, are specifically mentioned in only 5% of the RTAs. Various other specific measures which can, in principle, be integrated to either the national single window or the e-customs systems are mentioned in less than 5% of the RTAs, including e-payment systems or electronic systems for SPS certification or to obtain relevant import/ export permit or licenses.

Aside from Electronic exchange of TBT and financial information, our analysis shows that indeed "cross-border" paperless trade measures and provisions tend to be less readily featured in RTAs than "domestic" paperless trade measures. Provisions calling for "Mutual recognition of digital certificates and electronic signature", as well as "Promoting the cross-border electronic exchange of trade-related data and documents" are featured in roughly 20% of the RTAs with at least one paperless trade measure. Specific provisions related to "Electronic exchange of sanitary and phytosanitary (SPS) information" and to "certificates of origins (COOs)" are featured in 16% and 12% of these RTAs, respectively.

---

[20] See, e.g., Decision on a Paperless Environment for Customs and Trade by the European Parliament and the Council of the Council of the European Union (2008).

[21] For details, see Annex 2 of Yann Duval and Kong Menjing (2010). Digital trade Facilitation: Paperless trade in Regional Trade Agreements. Available from https://www.adb.org/publications/digital-trade-facilitation-paperless-trade-regional-trade-agreements

[22] As mentioned in table 2, e-exchange of TBT related information includes such methods as electronic mail, teleconferencing, videoconferencing (e.g., Australia-Republic of Korea FTA Art. 5.10).

Figure 3.4. Frequency of paperless trade measures and provision in regional trade agreements since 2005

Source: Authors' calculations
Note: The figure shows the percentage of RTAs (among the 90 containing at least one paperless trade measures) which feature provisions related to each of the paperless trade measures considered.

3.4. A closer look: paperless trade in selected RTAs in Asia-Pacific

The analysis presented above provided an overview of the type of paperless trade measures that are covered in RTAs and the extent to which RTAs signed by various countries emphasize paperless trade. In an effort to get deeper insights, we take a closer look at a small sample of recent regional trade agreements, selected for their particular emphasis of paperless trade issues and involving leading economies in South, South-East and East Asia and the Pacific (see table 3.3). The WTO TFA and the TPP are also included in the comparative analysis for reference.

Table 3.3. Status and Membership of Selected Asia-Pacific RTAs

Agreement name/Abbreviation	Year of entry into force	Membership
Singapore-India Comprehensive Economic Cooperation Agreement/SING-IND	2005	Singapore, India
Australia-Chile Free Trade Agreement/AUS-CHI	2009	Australia, Chile
Japan-Switzerland Economic Partnership Agreement/JAP-SWI	2009	Japan, Switzerland
Intra-ASEAN Agreements (including The ASEAN Trade in Goods Agreement, The ASEAN Agreement on Customs, Single Window Agreement)/ASEAN (ATIGA, AAC and SWA)	2010 (ASW since 2005; ATIGA since 2010)	Brunei Darussalam, Cambodia, Indonesia, Lao People's Democratic Republic, Malaysia, Myanmar, Philippines, Thailand, Viet Nam, Singapore
ASEAN-Australia-New Zealand Free Trade Agreement/AANZFTA	2010	ASEAN members, Australia, New Zealand
The United States-Republic of Korea Free Trade Agreement/US-KOR	2015	The United States, Republic of Korea
Republic of Korea-Viet Nam Free Trade Agreement/KOR-VN	2015	Republic of Korea, Viet Nam
Trans-pacific Partnership/TPP	Not yet in force (signed by all TPP members in 2015)	The United States, Australia, Brunei Darussalam, Chile, Malaysia, New Zealand, Peru, Singapore, and Viet Nam

Source: Authors' compilation

3.4.1. *"Paperless Trading" Articles*

As noted earlier, paperless trade measures are found in different chapters of an RTA, often as part of other substantive Articles or provisions. However, most recent RTAs also include one specific Article titled "Paperless Trading" or "Paperless Trade Administration". Before looking in more detail at the paperless trade coverage of our selected sample of Asia-Pacific RTAs, it is useful to review such Articles.

Table 3.4 shows the actual text of these Articles in the RTAs under review. All RTAs in our sample, with the exception of the intra-ASEAN agreements, include at least one article titled as such. These articles are generally found in e-commerce chapters, but not always. For example, the SING-IND places its "Paperless Trading" Article in the Customs Administration chapter, while the AUS-CHI Agreement features such Article in chapters of Customs Administration and Electronic Commerce. Regardless of the RTA considered, these Articles consistently promote the development and implementation of paperless trade systems among member states. However, details of commitments differ somewhat in substance and level of binding.

Most of the provisions in the "Paperless Trading" Articles are specified in non-binding terms. The two most commonly found provisions in the Articles are that parties will endeavour to (1) make electronic versions of their trade administration documents available publicly, and (2) accept trade documents submitted electronically as the legal equivalent of their paper version. Another provision often found is that they will (3) exchange views and/or cooperate with each other as well as internationally to enhance the acceptance of electronic documents. Interestingly, such cooperation provisions are often formulated as binding commitments. KOR-VN and AANZ also specifically commit "to work towards the implementation of initiatives which provide for the use of paperless trading", which may be interpreted as commitment to implement joint pilot projects in paperless trade.

Table 3.4. List of Paperless Trading provisions containing a binding framework

RTAs	Text of provisions entitled "Paperless Trading" or "Paperless Trade Administration"	Commitment level
AANZ	Art. 8(1) "Each Party *shall, where possible*, work towards the implementation of initiatives which provide for the use of paperless trading.	Non-binding
	Art. 8(2) "The Parties *shall* co-operate in international fora to enhance acceptance of electronic versions of trade administration documents."	Binding
	Art. 8(3) "The Parties *shall* exchange views and information on realizing, promoting and developments in paperless trading."	Binding
	Art. 8(4) "Each Party *shall endeavour* to make electronic versions of its trade administration documents publicly available."	Non-binding
JAP-SWI	Art. 79 "1. Each Party *shall endeavour* to make all trade administration documents available to the public in an electronic form.	Non-binding
	2. Each Party *shall endeavour* to accept trade administration documents submitted electronically as the legal equivalent of the paper versions of such documents.	Non-binding
	3. The Parties *shall* cooperate bilaterally and in international fora to enhance the acceptance of electronic versions of trade administration documents."	Binding
AUS-CHI	Art. 16.9(1) "1. Each Party *shall endeavour* to accept electronic versions of trade administration documents used by the other Party as the legal equivalent of paper documents, except where: (a) there is a domestic or international legal requirement to the contrary; or (b) doing so would reduce the effectiveness of the trade administration process."	Non-binding
	Art. 16.9(3) "Each Party *shall work towards* developing a single window to government incorporating relevant international standards for the conduct of trade administration, recognizing that each Party will have its own unique requirements and conditions."	
	Art. 5.11(1) "The Customs Administration of each Party, in implementing initiatives which provide for the use of paperless trading, *shall take into account* the methods agreed by the World Customs Organization, including adoption of the World Customs Organization data model for the simplification and harmonisation of data.	
	Art. 5.11(2) "The Customs Administration of each Party *shall work towards* having electronic means for all its customs reporting requirements, *as soon as practicable.*"	
	Art. 5.11(3) "The introduction and enhancement of information technology *shall, to the greatest extent possible*, be carried out in consultation with all relevant parties including businesses directly affected."	
SING-IND	Art. 4.4(1) "Recognising that trading using electronic filing and transfer of trade-related information and electronic versions of documents, as an alternative to paper-based methods will significantly enhance the efficiency of trade through reduction of cost and time, the Parties *shall co-operate* with a view to realising and promoting paperless trading between their respective customs administrations and its respective trading community.	Binding
	Art. 4.4(2) "The Parties *shall* exchange views and information on realizing, promoting and developments in paperless trading."	
KOR-US	Art. 15.6 "1. Each Party *shall endeavour* to make trade administration documents available to the public in electronic form.	Non-binding
	2. Each Party *shall endeavour* to accept trade administration documents submitted electronically as the legal equivalent of the paper version of those documents."	
KOR-VN	Art. 10.7 "1. Each Party *shall endeavour* to make electronic versions of its trade administration documents publicly available.	Non-binding
	2. Each Party *shall endeavour* to accept trade administration documents submitted electronically as the legal equivalent of the paper version of those documents.	
	3. Each Party *shall, where possible*, work towards the implementation of initiatives which provide for the use of paperless trading."	

Table 3.4. *(continued)*

RTAs	Text of provisions entitled "Paperless Trading" or "Paperless Trade Administration"	Commitment level
TPP	Art. 14.9 "Each Party *shall endeavour* to: (a) make trade administration documents available to the public in electronic form; and (b) accept trade administration documents submitted electronically as the legal equivalent of the paper version of those documents."	Non-binding

Source: Authors' compilation

AUS-CHI is the only agreement where the development of a single window for trade documents is specifically included under a "Paperless Trading" Article. One of the two such Articles featured in AUS-CHI also specifically refer to engaging in paperless trading taking into account the *"methods agreed by the World Customs Organization, including adoption of the World Customs Organization data model for the simplification and harmonisation of data".*

3.4.2. Paperless trade measures and commitments

On the basis of the typology of paperless trade measures developed earlier, table 3.5 provides an overview of the paperless trade coverage of each of the eight selected RTAs, including in terms of the level of commitment and details attached to each of the paperless trade measures featured. The table shows that paperless trade measures vary significantly across RTAs, both in substance and nature. However, with the exception of the India-Singapore Agreement, which entered into force over a decade ago (2005), all other RTAs included in the table have deeper coverage of paperless trade than the WTO TFA. The Australia-Chile (2009) Agreement appears to have been particularly pioneering for its time and still features some of the most binding and detailed paperless trade measures found in any RTA, including the TPP.

a. Measures related to acceptance of electronic copies

As noted earlier, this type of measure is commonly found in RTA articles titled "Paperless Trading" (see table 3.4). Referring to table 3.5, all eight RTAs examined have one or more dedicated provisions encouraging development and acceptance of electronic versions of trade administration documents. In contrast, the WTO TFA includes a specific provision on Acceptance of Copies (Art. 10.2), with all parties expected to *", where appropriate, endeavor to accept paper or electronic copies of supporting documents required for import, export or transit formalities."*

Going beyond simple encouragements, the ASEAN Single Window Agreement and its Protocol on the Legal Framework to Implement the ASEAN Single Window do provide for a framework for acceptance and legal recognition of electronic documents among member States. Such framework is indeed more elaborate and binding than those found in provisions of the other RTAs. In particular, Article 15 (Legal Effect of Electronic Documents, Data, and Information) of the Protocol indicate *that "Each Member State shall adopt procedures for authentication of NSW electronic documents, data, and information that shall be used or processed within the NSW and transmitted in an electronic form in the ASW environment." and that "Subject to national laws, rules and regulations of each Member State, authenticated* **electronic documents** *produced in connection with transactions under this Protocol may be admissible as evidence of any fact stated therein."*

b. Measures related to E-submission of trade-related documents

Such measures are typically found in the articles on "Release of Goods" and "Express Shipment" under chapters titled "Customs Administration and Trade Facilitation" or "Customs Procedures". Two of the eight RTAs include non-binding commitments to electronic submission of trade-related documents.

Table 3.5. Paperless trade coverage in selected Asia-Pacific agreements

Paperless trade measures / Agreement:	SING-IND	AUS-CHI	JAP-SWI	Intra-ASEAN	AANZ FTA	KOR-US	KOR-VN	TPP	WTO TFA
Year of entry into force:	2005	2009	2009	2010	2010	2012	2015	–	–
Acceptance of electronic copies	*	**	**	**	***	**	**	**	*
E-submission of trade-related documents						*	*	*	*
E-Submission of Air Cargo Manifests						*	*	*	
E-system of Export or Import Permits									
E-system for SPS certification								*	
E-system of COO						*		*	
Electronic record-keeping	*	***			*	*		*	
E-payment system								***	*
Electronic/Automated Customs System/ Customs Automation		*		*	**	***	**	***	
Automated System for Risk Management and targeting					**	***	***	***	
Electronic Single Window System		***		***				**	*
E-system for inter-organization communication	*			*					
Laws for electronic transactions	*	***	**		**		**	***	
Promoting e-certification and e-signatures		*	*	*	*	*	*	*	
Mutual determination of authentication technologies		***			*	*	*	*	
Proving in court legal compliance of E-authentication		*	*		*	*	*	*	
Meeting standards for E-signature and E-authentication			**			**		*	
Mutual recognition of digital certificates and E-signature		***	**		**		**	*	
Interoperability of digital certificates used by business		*			*		*		
Trade-related electronic data exchange	*			***ⁱ		**	**	***	
E-exchange of COO related information				*ⁱ					
E-exchange of SPS related information				*ⁱ				*	
E-exchange of TBT related information		**		*ⁱ		**	*	**	
E-transmission of financial information			*		*	**		*	
International standards for paperless trade		*	*	*	*	*	*	*	*
Total number of paperless trade measures:	5	12	8	10	12	15	14	21	5

Source: Authors' compilation

Notes: 1 star (*) indicates the measure is only mentioned, generally as an option, without further clarification; 2 stars (**) indicate the measure is encouraged (e.g., Shall endeavour to; or Shall, to the extent possible, to) with clarification on how it is to be provided/implemented (e.g. complying with relevant international standards); 3 stars (***) indicate that implementation of the measures is required and binding (e.g., shall) with details included on how to do so. ⁱ indicates that commitment to these measures is implied by the existence of the regional ASEAN Single Window Agreement itself.

Electronic submission is urged in KOR-US and TPP, and is encouraged in the WTO TFA. For example, KOR-US Article 7.2 requires members to *"provide for customs information to be submitted and processed electronically before the goods arrive in order for them to be released on their arrival"*. In the WTO TFA, the country's situation and capacity are considered through the words *"as appropriate"* when encouraging states to *"provide for advance lodging of documents in electronic formats"*.

Electronic submission of (air cargo) manifest is specifically promoted in several agreements. For instance, in the article on "Express Shipment" in TPP, parties shall *"allow a single submission of information covering all goods contained in an express shipment, such as a manifest, through, if possible, electronic means"*.

c. Measures related to E-system for SPS certification

Such measures are usually found in RTA chapters dedicated to "Sanitary and Phytosanitary Measures", when they exist. Only one of the eight RTAs specifically refers to the potential goal of developing an electronic system for SPS certification.

TPP indicates that *"the Parties shall promote the implementation of electronic certification and other technologies to facilitate trade"* in its Article 7.12 on Certification.

d. Measures related to E-system for Certificates of Origin (COO)

Paperless trade measures related to COO are usually found in chapters on "Rules of Origin and Origin Procedures". Development of electronic systems for COO is implied in two of the agreements.

KOR-US provides for electronic certification as one option. Specifically, an importer under KOR-US can claim preferential tariff treatment based on *"either a written or electronic certification by the importer, exporter, or producer"*. In TPP, a Committee on Rules of Origin and Origin Procedures will be established and *"consult on the technical aspects of submission and the format of the electronic certification of origin"*.

e. Measures related to electronic record-keeping

This type of measure is usually found in the Article on "Records" or "Record Keeping Requirements" under the chapter of "Rules of Origin and Origin Procedures", as documents subject to electronic record-keeping requirements in RTAs are related to COO issues in most cases. Five of the RTAs provide for electronic-record keeping, but only three have specific provisions related to this measure in their Rules of Origin chapters.

In AUS-CHI, the members are obliged to keep electronic records (Article 4.20). However, in KOR-US (Article 6.17 on "Record Keeping Requirements") and TPP (Article 3.26), e-record keeping is only one of several options: *"any medium that allows for prompt retrieval, including electronic, optical, magnetic or written form in accordance with that Party's law"* could be chosen by members. The WTO TFA does not include any mention of electronic record-keeping.

f. Measures related to E-payment system

This type of measure is not generally featured in RTAs. While the WTO TFA Article 7.2 has a separate provision on electronic payment indicating that, *"to the extent practicable"*, members shall *"adopt or maintain procedures allowing the option of electronic payment for duties, taxes, fees, and charges collected by customs incurred upon importation and exportation"*, such specific measure related to payment to customs is absent from any of the eight RTAs reviewed.

However, electronic payment is provided for in a very detailed way in TPP in the chapter on "Financial Services" – with no particular focus on BtoG transactions. TPP member States are committed to providing the supply of electronic payment services for payment card transactions among members. It not only conditions the cross-border supply of this electronic payment service, but also sets clear limits to the supply scope, with the exclusion of the transfer of funds to and from transactors' accounts, the exclusive use of proprietary networks to process, and on business to business basis. In addition, the section also provides for public policy exception to the supply of such electronic payment.

g. Measures related to electronic/automated customs system

The measures "electronic/automated customs system" and "automated system for risk management and targeting" are often found in the article of "Automation" under the chapter of "Customs Procedures". The majority of the agreements reviewed (6 of 8 RTAs) encourage establishing or developing electronic/automated customs systems, while 4 provide specifically for risk management.

As can be seen in box 3.1, making electronic systems accessible to customs users is a binding commitment in both KOR-VN (Article 4.3) and KOR-US (Article 7.3), as well as in TPP (Article 5.6). In contrast, the related provision in AUS-CHI (Article 5.11), which is included in an Article on "Paperless Trading" has greater scope but is of a "best endeavour" nature. It also has the particularity to stress the importance of consulting with stakeholders, including businesses, in developing the electronic systems.

Box 3.1. Selected Articles relating to E-Customs System/Customs Automation

KOR-US

Article 7.3: Automation

Each Party shall use information technology that expedites procedures for the release of goods and shall:

(a) make *electronic systems* accessible to customs users;

(b) endeavour to use international standards;

(c) endeavour to develop *electronic systems* that are compatible with the other Party's systems, in order to facilitate bilateral exchange of international trade data; and

(d) endeavour to develop a set of common data elements and processes in accordance with World Customs Organization (WCO) Customs Data Model and related WCO recommendations and guidelines.

Article 7.4: Risk Management

Each Party shall adopt or maintain *electronic or automated risk management systems* for assessment and targeting that enable its customs authority to focus its inspection activities on high-risk goods and that simplify the clearance and movement of low-risk goods.

TPP

Article 5.6: Automation

1. Each Party shall:

   (a) endeavour to use international standards with respect to procedures for the release of goods;

   (b) make electronic systems accessible to customs users;

   (c) employ electronic or automated systems for risk analysis and targeting;

   (d) endeavour to implement common standards and elements for import and export data in accordance with the World Customs Organization (WCO) Data Model;

   (e) take into account, as appropriate, WCO standards, recommendations, models and methods developed through the WCO or APEC; and

   (f) work toward developing a set of common data elements that are drawn from the WCO Data Model and related WCO recommendations as well as guidelines to facilitate government to government electronic sharing of data for purposes of analyzing trade flows.

2. Each Party shall endeavour to provide a facility that allows importers and exporters to electronically complete standardised import and export requirements at a single entry point.

With regard to "Automated System for Risk Management and Targeting", it is made a requirement in the two KOR agreements as well as the TPP. However, the TPP language is more concise and the measure is included as part of the article on "Automation" (Article 5.6), which also covers the setting up of a single window.

h. Measures related to electronic single window

Measures on single window are most commonly found in chapters dedicated to customs procedures and trade facilitation, although at least one RTA mentions such measures in its e-commerce chapter. Three of the eight RTAs refer to the need to establish single window facilities.

AUS-CHI mentions the establishment of single window in Article 16.9 ("Paperless Trading") under the chapter of Electronic Commerce. In TPP, the term "single window" is not used but the need to develop such facility is specified in the last provision of the article on "Automation" (Article 5.6) of the Customs and trade facilitation chapter: *"Each Party shall endeavour to provide a facility that allows importers and exporters to electronically complete standardised import and export requirements at a single entry point."* In contrast, the WTO TFA features a dedicated "Single Window" article, with members expected to endeavour to maintain such facility and use information technology to support it *"to the extent possible and practicable"*.

Among all RTAs, intra-ASEAN agreements have a special emphasis on electronic single window. Article 49 of the ATIGA indeed binds ASEAN members to take measures to establish not only a national but a regional single window, with specific implementation agreements and protocols providing details of what is to be done (see box 3.2).

Box 3.2. Selected Articles relating to Single Window

ASEAN Trade in Good Agreement

Article 49: Establishment of the ASEAN Single Window

Member States shall undertake necessary measures to establish and operate their respective *National Single Windows* and *the ASEAN Single Window* in accordance with the provisions of the *Agreement to Establish and Implement the ASEAN Single Window* and the *Protocol to Establish and Implement the ASEAN Single Window*.

WTO TFA

Article 10.4: Single Window

4.1 Members shall endeavour to establish or maintain *a single window*, enabling traders to submit documentation and/or data requirements for importation, exportation, or transit of goods through a single entry point to the participating authorities or agencies. After the examination by the participating authorities or agencies of the documentation and/or data, the results shall be notified to the applicants through the single window in a timely manner.

[..]

4.4 Members shall, to the extent possible and practicable, use information technology to support the *single window*.

---

i. Measures related to laws for electronic transactions

Provisions related to establishment of laws for electronic transactions are consistently found in Electronic Commerce chapters of RTAs, typically under a specific Article focusing on domestic regulations. Six of the RTAs reviewed include such provisions, although they differ in substance.

As can be seen in box 3.3, the JAP-SWI agreement (Article 77 on Domestic Regulation) provides for the most general provision, only calling for transparent administration of e-commerce and the need for regulations not be burdensome, on a best endeavour basis. Other RTAs are more specific and both KOR-VN and TPP provisions refer specifically to UNCITRAL instruments.

While the KOR-VN only encourages parties to take such instruments into account, the TPP requires that member states' domestic regulations regarding electronic transaction *"shall be consistent with"* the principles of the UNCITRAL Model Law on Electronic Commerce 1996 or the United Nations Electronic Communications Convention, 2005. A similar reference to the e-CC is contained in the ASEAN Legal Protocol to the Single Window. The provisions regarding laws on electronic transactions in AUS-CHI are also stated in a more detailed way, setting various principles to be followed by parties in developing legislation in this area. The special emphasis on supporting *"industry-led development of electronic commerce"* is worth noting in this regard.

Box 3.3. Selected Articles relating to Laws for Electronic Transactions

JAP-SWI

Article 77: Domestic Regulation

Each Party shall endeavour to ensure that all its measures affecting electronic commerce are administered in a transparent, objective, reasonable and impartial manner, and are not more burdensome than necessary.

KOR-VN

Article 10.4: Domestic Regulatory Framework

Each Party shall endeavour to adopt or maintain its domestic laws and regulations governing electronic transactions taking into account the UNCITRAL Model Law on Electronic Commerce 1996.

AUS-CHI

Article 16.5: Domestic Electronic Transaction Frameworks

1. Each Party shall adopt or maintain measures regulating electronic transactions based on the following principles:
   (a) a transaction including a contract shall not be denied legal effect, validity or enforceability solely on the grounds that it is in the form of an electronic communication; and
   (b) laws should not discriminate arbitrarily between different forms of technology.
2. Nothing in paragraph 1 prevents the Parties from making exceptions in their domestic laws to the general principles outlined in that paragraph.
3. Each Party shall:
   (a) minimize the regulatory burden on electronic commerce; and
   (b) ensure that its measures regulating electronic commerce support industry-led development of electronic commerce.

TPP

Article 14.5: Domestic Electronic Transactions Framework

1. Each Party shall maintain a legal framework governing electronic transactions consistent with the principles of the UNCITRAL Model Law on Electronic Commerce 1996 or the United Nations Convention on the Use of Electronic Communications in International Contracts, done at New York, November 23, 2005.
2. Each Party shall endeavour to:
   (a) avoid any unnecessary regulatory burden on electronic transactions; and
   (b) facilitate input by interested persons in the development of its legal framework for electronic transactions.

j. Measures related to promoting e-certification and e-signature

These measures are typically found in the articles titled "Electronic Authentication" and/or "Electronic Signature"[23] under the chapter of Electronic Commerce. All eight RTAs reviewed feature some more or less specific provisions in this area.

SING-IND does not feature detailed provisions on electronic authentication and electronic signature, nor does the WTO TFA. In contrast, other RTAs generally seek to promote acceptance and mutual recognition of electronic authentication and signatures, including by encouraging the parties to maintain flexible and technology neutral laws and regulations in this area. In KOR-US and TPP, this is done by specifying what type of legislation parties should *not* adopt, e.g., laws that would *"prohibit parties to an electronic transaction from mutually determining the appropriate authentication methods for that transaction"* (TPP Article 14.6) or *"deny a signature legal validity solely on the basis that the signature is in electronic form"* (KOR-US Article 15.4).

KOR-VN and AUS-CHI Agreements take a more "positive" approach with the relevant articles instead indicating that *"shall adopt or maintain measures regulating electronic authentication"* (AUS-CHI Article 16.6) that would, for example, permit parties to mutually determine the appropriate authentication

---

[23] Articles on e-transaction laws which reference UNCITRAL instruments also indirectly cover these issues. In many cases, the RTA Articles on "e-signature" simply restate key underlying principles of UNCITRAL texts.

methods and *"not limit the recognition of authentication technologies or implementation models"* (KOR-VN Article 10.3).[24] Both Agreements also commit parties to work towards the mutual recognition of digital certificates and electronic signature at the governmental level, and based on international standards, suggesting a higher level of overall commitment that in many other RTAs. Interoperability of electronic authentication and/or digital certificates is also encouraged in both the agreements, as well as in the TPP.

k. Measures related to trade-related electronic data exchange

"Trade-related electronic data exchange" among parties, or cross-border paperless trade, is often promoted under the Articles of "Paperless Trading" in E-commerce chapters or "Automation" in Customs chapters. Five of the RTAs reviewed include related provisions.

Commitments in this area are typically on a best endeavour basis, with the notable exception of ASEAN, which features binding and detailed commitments on electronic exchange of data among members under its ASEAN Single Window (ASW) Agreement.

Among the other agreements reviewed, KOR-US, KOR-VN and TPP stand out in terms of making references to specific international standards *"to facilitate bilateral exchange of international trade data"* (KOR-US Article 7.3). For example, in Article 5.6 on Automation, TPP Parties are committed to *"work toward developing a set of common data elements that are drawn from the WCO Data Model and related WCO recommendations as well as guidelines to facilitate government to government electronic sharing of data for purposes of analysing trade flows"*. While JAP-SWI, AUS-CHI and AANZ may not feature direct provisions on exchanging trade-related data electronically, an implicit commitment to it is made in *"Paperless Trading"* Articles, which all include a provision that *"Parties shall cooperate bilaterally [...] to enhance the acceptance of electronic versions of trade administration documents."*

With regard to the four sub-measures, they are often specified under the specific chapters of "Rules of Origin and Origin Procedures", "Sanitary and Phytosanitary Measures", "Barriers to Trade" and "Financial Service" respectively. TPP is the only Agreement which has a specific commitment to exchange of information on SPS issues by electronic means, although it is limited to *"possible"* cases. In contrast, electronic exchange of TBT-related information is discussed in several agreements, although again on a *"best endeavour"* basis.

Among the RTAs reviewed in detail, four agreements (US-KOR, JAP-SWI, AANZ and TPP) cover the electronic exchange of financial information. JAP-SWI uses "negative" language and states that: *"Neither party shall take measures that prevent transfers of information into or out of its Area or the processing of financial information, including transfers of data by electronic means" where such transfers [...] are necessary for the conduct of the ordinary business of a financial supplier of the other party"*. In the chapter of financial services, the TPP urges members to allow electronic exchange of financial information, with an exception for protecting personal information and a requirement of obtaining prior authorization.

l. Measures related to international standards for paperless trade

Measures related to the use of international standards for paperless trade are normally found either in Articles on "Automation" in Customs chapters, or in "Paperless Trading" Articles in e-commerce chapters. All but one of the RTAs reviewed, as well as the WTO TFA, refer to and/or take into account international standards when implementing various paperless trade measures.

For example, parties in TPP and KOR-VN shall *"endeavour to use international standards"* when automating customs systems. The "Paperless Trading" Article in AUS-CHI refers to the need to establish single window by *"incorporating relevant internationals standards"*. The ASEAN ATIGA Article 58 on "Application of Information Technology" also states that *"Member States, where applicable, shall apply information technology in customs operations based on internationally accepted standards for expeditious customs clearance and release of goods."*

---

[24]   This provision reflects the principle of "technology neutrality" featured in UNCITRAL text as well as the new FA-PT text.

As noted earlier, some paperless trade provisions go a step further and mention specific standards or conventions and recommendations to guide implementation – in particular in the TPP. In contrast, while the WTO TFA has a dedicated article on 'Use of International Standards' (Article 10.3) in regulating formalities of importation, exportation, and transit, it is not specifically related to application of information technology and does not specify a set of standards or recommendations. It does, however, encourage parties to use and prepare and review periodically relevant international standards and establish a committee which works towards the implementation of international standards.

3.4.3. Linkages with the Framework Agreement on Facilitation of Cross-border Paperless Trade in Asia and the Pacific

The "Framework Agreement on Facilitation of Cross-border Paperless Trade in Asia and the Pacific" (FA-PT) opened for signature on 1 October 2016, as the newest UN treaty in the area of trade and development.[25] The FA-PT is not an regional trade agreement in the common sense of the term, as it does not include any trade liberalization commitments and focuses solely on enabling cross-border trade-related electronic data exchange among parties. It has been described as a regional "digital complement" to the WTO Trade Facilitation Agreement.[26] Developed and negotiated by ESCAP member States following adoption of a resolution on *Enabling Paperless Trade [...] for inclusive and sustainable intraregional trade facilitation* in 2012,[27] it can be expected to provide a supportive and dedicated framework to accelerate the harmonized implementation of paperless trade commitments made by ESCAP members States with each other through RTAs (see box 3.4).

Box 3.4. Objective of the Framework Agreement on Facilitation of Cross-border Paperless Trade in Asia and the Pacific

Article 1 Objective

The objective of the present Framework Agreement is to promote cross-border paperless trade by enabling the exchange and mutual recognition of trade-related data and documents in electronic form and facilitating interoperability among national and subregional single windows and/or other paperless trade systems, for the purpose of making international trade transactions more efficient and transparent while improving regulatory compliance.

A review of the provisions of the FA-PT against the paperless trade measures and provisions in the selected RTAs confirms indeed that the FA-PT guiding principles are not only consistent with those found in RTA, but that participation in the FA-PT could indeed help countries fulfil or better implement several of their RTA commitments. For example, as noted earlier, a common provision in "Paperless Trading" articles in RTAs is that parties will exchange views and/or cooperate with each other as well as internationally to enhance the acceptance of electronic documents. Participation in the FA-PT would readily meet RTA partners' commitment to cooperate internationally on paperless trade. In particular, one of the most far reaching components of the FA-PT is Article 8 on "Cross-border mutual recognition of trade-related data and documents in electronic form." Implementation of this provision is expected to potentially enable the electronic exchange and legal recognition of various trade-related data and documents such as electronic COO, SPS certificates and TBT certificates, as envisaged in various RTAs.

Some RTAs (e.g., KOR-VN and AANZ) also commit parties to *"work towards the implementation of initiatives which provide for the use of paperless trading"*. FA-PT Article 13 on "Pilot projects and sharing of lessons learned", where *"The Parties shall endeavour to initiate and launch pilot projects on cross-border exchange of trade-related data and documents in electronic form"* would certainly support implementation of such RTA commitments.

---

[25] Any of the 53 Member States of the United Nations Economic and Social Commission for Asia and the Pacific (ESCAP) may become a party. See: http://www.unescap.org/resources/framework-agreement-facilitation-cross-border-paperless-trade-asia-and-pacific

[26] http://www.tfafacility.org/new-un-treaty-facilitate-paperless-trade-asia-and-pacific-support-trade-facilitation-agreement

[27] ESCAP (2012). ESCAP Resolution 68/3: Enabling paperless trade and the cross-border recognition of electronic data and documents for inclusive and sustainable intraregional trade facilitation. Available from http://www.unescap.org/resources/escap-resolution-683-enabling-paperless-trade-and-cross-border-recognition-electronic-data

Importantly, our analysis of RTAs revealed that implementation of paperless trade on the basis of international standards was one of the most common features and provisions among agreements that did address paperless trade issues. Such an approach is also consistent with that of the FA-PT Article 9 on "International Standards for exchange of trade-related data and documents in electronic form", stating that parties *"shall endeavour to apply international standards and guidelines in order to ensure interoperability in paperless trade and to develop safe, secure and reliable means of communication for the exchange of data"*, as well as *"endeavour to become involved in the development of international standards and best practices related to cross-border paperless trade."* The first four "General Principles" (Article 5) of the FA-PT – *(a) Functional equivalence; (b) Non-discrimination of the use of electronic communications; (c) Technological neutrality; (d) Promotion of interoperability* – are in particular directly related to those established and promoted in United Nations Commission on International Trade Law (UNCITRAL) instruments referred to in several RTA provisions related to legislation on electronic transaction and/or e-signatures.[28]

Building on these intentional standards and principles, the FA-PT provides more details on how some of the paperless trade provisions in RTAs may be implemented. For example, on single window, the FA-PT does not only encourage parties to establish single windows, as the WTO TFA and several RTAs already do, but encourage them to *"use them for cross-border paperless trade"*. It also provides an intergovernmental and institutional framework to do so, with establishment of a Paperless Trade Council and working groups, and the development of individual and regional action plans. Looking forward, Parties may reflect relevant commitments made through RTAs in these action plans.

3.5. Conclusion

The analysis presented in this paper reveals that the number of paperless trade measures in RTAs entered into force globally since 2005 essentially doubled, with a large majority of RTAs now featuring one or more measures aiming to exchange trade-related data and information electronically. In many cases, recent RTAs are found to go further than the WTO TFA in promoting digital trade facilitation and the application of modern information and communications technologies to trade procedures – with the possible exception of e-payment of duties and fees, which is not specifically mentioned in any of the RTAs reviewed. While 30 of the 138 RTAs reviewed feature one or more articles dedicated to "Paperless Trading" or "Paperless Trade Administration", provisions related to more specific paperless trade measures are found in different chapters, including but not limited to chapters on Customs and trade facilitation as well as on e-commerce.

Many of the recent RTAs in Asia and the Pacific implicitly or explicitly call upon the parties to develop electronic exchange of trade-related data and documents and work towards interoperability of paperless trade systems. However, they provide little detail on how to do so beyond recommending cooperation among the parties taking into account existing international standards and tools. In this context, the new UN *Framework Agreement on Facilitation of Cross-border Paperless Trade in Asia and the Pacific* (FA-PT) provides a useful multilateral framework through which paperless trade-related RTA commitments may be concretized.

Looking forward, more research may be undertaken on the extent to which countries have implemented the various paperless trade measures they have committed to through RTAs. Preliminary evidence points to countries having achieved partial implementation at best. Even in the case of ASEAN, which has shown strong (binding) commitments to cross-border paperless trade through ATIGA and its related ASEAN Single Window Agreement, implementation has been much slower than expected. In this context, the new FA-PT stands as a potentially useful tool for RTA members to share experience and cooperate with a wider set of trade partners committed to paperless trade, providing new knowledge and renewed impetus to accelerate implementation of RTA commitments.

Further efforts may also be useful in refining the typology of paperless trade measures and provisions proposed in this paper. Similarly, more work may be needed to improve the accuracy of the RTA ratings in terms of depth of coverage and commitments to paperless trade, in particular by more fully taking into account the nature and level of bindings of each provision across a larger set of agreements.

---

[28] See Castellani et al. (2017) for a recent discussion of these instruments.

References

Castellani, L., Wu, M., and Botwright, K. (2017). Making Deals in Cyberspace: What's the Problem? Available at http://www3.weforum.org/docs/WEF_White_Paper_Making_Deals_in_Cyberspace.pdf

ECE-WEF (2017). Paperless Trading: How does it impact the trade system? Available at http://www3.weforum.org/docs/WEF_36073_paperless_Trading_How_Doos_It_Impact_the_Trading_System.pdf

ECSG Chair (2004). *"APEC's Strategies and Actions Toward A Cross-Border Paperless Trading Environment"*. Asia-Pacific Economic Cooperation. 2004/AMM/004, Chili, Vol. 4, pp.1-6. Available at http://www.apec.org/~/media/Files/Press/Features/2007/04_amm_004.pdf

ESCAP. (2016). "Framework Agreement on Facilitation of Cross-border Paperless Trade in Asia and the Pacific", in ESCAP, Resolution adopted by the Economic and Social Commission for Asia and the Pacific, (E/ESCAP/RES/72/4). United Nations. Available at http://www.un.org/ga/search/view_doc.asp?symbol=E/ESCAP/RES/72/4&Lang=E

Laryea, E. (2002). *Paperless Trade: Opportunity, Challenges and Solutions.* Kluwer Law International, Deventer, pp.1-2.

Laryea, E. (2005). "Facilitating Paperless International Trade: A Survey of Law and Policy in Asia", *International Review of Law Computers & Technology*, Vol. 19, No. 2, pp. 121-142.

Monteiro, J.A., and Teh, R. (2017). Provisions on Electronic Commerce in Regional Trade Agreements. WTO Working Paper ERSD-2017-11. Available at https://www.wto.org/english/res_e/reser_e/ersd201711_e.pdf

Shepherd, B., and Duval, Y. (2015). "Estimating the benefits of cross-border paperless trade in Asia and the Pacific", Chapter V in Reducing Trade Costs in Asia-Pacific Developing Countries, ESCAP Studies in Trade and Investment No. 84, United Nations, Bangkok.

United Nations Network of Experts for Paperless Trade and Transport in Asia and the Pacific (UNNExT), UNNExT Policy Briefs, Various issues. Available at https://unnext.unescap.org

Wu, M. (2017). Digital Trade-related Provisions in Regional Trade Agreements: Existing Models and Lessons from Multilateral Trade System. RTA Exchange. Geneva: International Centre for Trade and Sustainable Development (ICTSD) and the Inter-American Development Bank (IDB). Available at http://e15initiative.org/wp-content/uploads/2015/09/RTA-Exchange-Digital-Trade-Mark-Wu-Final.pdf

Chapter 4

The Framework Agreement on Facilitation of Cross-border Paperless Trade in Asia and the Pacific: An inclusive platform towards digital trade facilitation

On 19 May 2016, the *Framework Agreement on Facilitation of Cross-border Paperless Trade in Asia and the Pacific* (FA-PT) was adopted by the United Nations Economic and Social Commission for Asia and the Pacific (ESCAP), making it the newest UN treaty in the area of trade and development. The Framework is fully dedicated to the digitalization of trade processes and enabling the seamless electronic exchange and legal recognition of trade-related data and documents across borders, rather than only between stakeholders located in the same country. Implementation of the Agreement is expected to greatly reduce transaction time and costs as well as increase regulatory compliance.[1]

Developed by a diverse group of more than 25 Asia-Pacific economies at very different stages of development over four years, the Framework Agreement is designed as an inclusive and enabling platform that will benefit all participating economies regardless of where they stand in terms of trade facilitation implementation. While the preparatory work has been spear-headed by Republic of Korea, Bangladesh was the first to announce Cabinet approval for the signing of the Agreement. Bangladesh, Cambodia and China formally signed the new treaty at a special ceremony in Bangkok on 29 August 2017. The Agreement will enter into force after five member States ratify it.

Achieving cross-border paperless trade across the region is expected to be a long and difficult process, and it cannot be achieved without close collaboration between countries. The Framework Agreement is expected to support that process by providing a dedicated institutional framework for countries with proven political will to develop legal and technical solutions for cross-border paperless trade, including through pilot projects, capacity building and technical assistance. Full implementation of cross-border paperless trade is expected to help reduce export costs by up to 31% across the region, and reduce export time by over 40% from current levels. Annual additional export potential from such time and cost savings have been estimated at $257 billion for the whole region.

The FA-PT provides a unique tool for countries to better implement the World Trade Organization Trade Facilitation Agreement (WTO TFA), taking full advantage of emerging digital solutions and technologies (ADB, 2017). It is also expected to help countries meet commitments they have already made on paperless trade through regional trade agreements (RTAs) and other agreements. Importantly, the FA-PT promotes existing international standards, tools and instruments, including those of the UN Commission on International Trade Law (UNCITRAL), who provided substantive support for the development of the Framework throughout the process, as well as those of the United Nations Centre for Trade Facilitation and Electronic Business (UN/CEFACT) and the World Customs Organization (WCO).

According to the results of the 2017 United Nations Global Survey on Trade Facilitation and Paperless Trade Implementation, significant progress has been made in implementing measures specified in the WTO TFA (ADB and ESCAP, 2017). However, measures related to automation of trade procedures and use of electronic data and documents are still lagging in implementation in many economies. Such paperless trade measures are important tools and "digital" complements for better implementation of the WTO TFA and the development of cross-border e-commerce.

Despite existing efforts and initiatives, the results highlight the difficulties for the region in moving towards cross-border paperless trade: the average implementation rate of such measures (e.g, including electronic exchange of Certificates of Origin, or of Sanitary and Phyto-Sanitary Certificates) stand at less than 20%, compared to more than 50% for most other types of trade facilitation measures. This makes

---

[1]   See also Xue (2017), for an alternative discussion of the FA-PT.

the FA-PT both relevant and timely: it will provide the institutional foundation for member States to cooperate and accelerate progress in this area, ultimately bolstering competitiveness of participating economies and enabling them to benefit fully from the digital economy.

4.1. An Overview of the Framework Agreement

The potential benefits from conducting trade transactions on the basis of electronic rather than paper-based data and documentation have long been recognized by a number of Asian and Pacific countries, who began implementing paperless trade systems from the late 1990s and early 2000s. The economic gains from early implementation of such systems have been significant, as in the cases of the Republic of Korea and Singapore.[2] To date, most of the paperless trade systems in the region have focused on facilitating information exchange between stakeholders domestically. As a result, the flow of electronic trade information generated domestically encounters both technical and legal barriers beyond the border, requiring traders to maintain conventional paper-based trade practices, thus reducing the overall benefits and return on investment from paperless trade systems.

In that context, the objective of the FA-PT is to "*promote cross-border paperless trade by enabling the exchange and mutual recognition of trade-related data and documents in electronic form and facilitating interoperability among national and subregional single windows and/or other paperless trade systems, for the purpose of making international trade transactions more efficient and transparent while improving regulatory compliance* (Article 1)." To do so, it provides parties an enabling and structured intergovernmental framework to work together on addressing the complex issues associated with cross-border paperless trade.

The FA-PT contains a preamble and 25 articles (see box 4.1). It has the following key features:

1. A set of key principles to promote connectivity and trade facilitation, including functional equivalence, promotion of interoperability, improved trade facilitation and regulatory compliance, and cooperation between public and private sectors.

2. A multi-layered institutional arrangement as an operating platform: a Council at high level as a decision-making body; a Standing Committee at senior official level as an operative body; and Working Groups, at expert level, as substantive supportive bodies.

Box 4.1. Structure of the Framework Agreement (FA-PT)

The Framework Agreement contains a preamble (providing the background and rationale for the arrangement) and 25 articles. Articles 1 to 16 are substantive clauses, covering objective, scope, definitions, general principles and other action-oriented measures, while articles 17 to 25 are final clauses, specifying standard provisions typical of a UN treaty. Key substantive articles are as follows:

Article 5:   General principles

Article 6:   National Policy Framework, Enabling Domestic Legal Environment and Paperless Trade Committee

Article 7:   Facilitation of Cross-border Paperless Trade and Development of national Single Window(s)

Article 8:   Cross-border Mutual Recognition of Trade-related Data and Documents in Electronic Form

Article 9:   International Standards for Exchange of Trade-related Data and Documents in Electronic Form

Article 10: Relation with Other Legal Instruments Enabling Cross-border Paperless Trade

Article 11: Institutional Arrangements

Article 12: Action Plan

Article 13: Pilot Projects and Sharing of Lessons Learned

Article 14: Capacity Building

Source: http://www.unescap.org/resources/framework-agreement-facilitation-cross-border-paperless-trade-asia-and-pacific

---

[2] See United Nations Network of Experts for Paperless Trade and Transport in Asia and the Pacific (UNNExT), UNNExT Policy Briefs, Various issues. Available from https://unnext.unescap.org/policy-briefs

3. A commitment to enabling mutual recognition of trade-related data and documents: mutual recognition would be provided on the basis of a substantially equivalent level of reliability, to be mutually agreed upon by the parties through the Institutional Arrangement of the Framework Agreement. Implementation of such mutual recognition may involve bilateral and subregional arrangements at the operational level.

4. A comprehensive action plan to address legal and technical issues in cross-border paperless trade, to be developed and implemented by the parties. It will include development of technical and legal measures, detailed actions for designing pilot projects, capacity building support and information and experience sharing activities among members, etc.

The collective implementation of the action plan is expected to result in the emergence of practical standardized solutions and protocols for cross-border paperless trade.

4.2. Benefits of the Framework Agreement

Implementation of cross-border paperless trade in Asia and the Pacific is expected to reduce export costs by 15-30% on average, increasing the annual export potential of the region by $257 billion when fully implemented (Shepherd and Duval, 2015). Total direct cost savings due to implementation at the country level are economically significant, with, for example, Sri Lanka total transaction costs expected to decrease by $240 million annually. The expected benefits for ESCAP member States who become parties to the FA-PT can be summarized as follows:

1. Accelerated progress towards a paperless trade environment at the national level on the basis of the political will demonstrated during the accession process to the FA-PT.

2. Opportunity to integrate emerging cross-border paperless trade considerations and best practices early in the development of national single window and other paperless trade systems to ensure they are interoperable and enabled for (future) cross-border data exchange, in particular through structured and regular sharing of lessons.

3. Reduction in overall investment costs and maximization of return from investments in paperless trade systems, through concurrent development of national paperless trade systems and environment for cross-border trade data exchange.

4. Ready access to potential counterpart countries interested to negotiate and achieve cross-border data exchange, avoiding or reducing needs for engaging in numerous and/or potentially incompatible bilateral initiatives.

5. Direct participation in the development of pragmatic solutions for the cross-border exchange of trade documents, with opportunity for countries with relevant experience and existing practices to ensure that new regional systems and solutions will be harmonized and interoperable with what they have already achieved on a bilateral and/or subregional basis. For less advanced parties, such direct participation may be expected to increase national capacity and the possibility of becoming early adopter/implementer.

6. Compliance with commitments the party may have made through in its bilateral and plurilateral trade agreements to collaborate on exchanging electronic of data and documents (typically featured in "Paperless Trading" articles in RTAs, or related provisions).

7. Ultimately: (a) reduced trade transaction time and costs, potentially boosting trade competitiveness; (b) improved levels of compliance by traders to regulatory requirements in international trade; and (c) more direct engagement of small and medium-size enterprise (SMEs) in international trade and cross-border e-commerce.

As noted earlier, the objective of the FA-PT is to facilitate cross-border trade data exchange between member States and enable mutual recognition of electronic trade data and documents, but it is in no way to make electronic data exchange mandatory among parties. States which sign the FA-PT will, however, have some obligations. For example, they are expected to actively participate in the institutional arrangement under the Agreement (e.g., the Paperless Trade Council and Standing Committee once a year), and to participate in the development and implementation of collective and individual actions towards paperless trade based on their available resources and capacities. Importantly, there are no technical or legal pre-requisite to becoming a party of the Framework Agreement, as assessments of legal and technical gap will be done by the parties as part of the implementation of the Framework.[3]

4.3. Conclusion

Cross-border paperless trade could be a source of great trade gains. It has the potential to make trade not only more transparent but also more inclusive. Paperless trade is at the cross-road between trade facilitation and e-commerce, enabling Government to Government (GtoG) and Government to Business (GtoB) information and documents exchange without which cross-border e-commerce will not flourish, greatly limiting SMEs ability to directly engage in trade with customers outside their country.

Entry into force and implementation of the FA-PT would address the lack of an intergovernmental coordination mechanism to support adoption of common international standards, harmonize legal frameworks and gradually fill the capacity gap and build understanding and trust between countries so that all trade stakeholders can effectively exchange data across borders in a reliable and safe environment. Five member States of ESCAP need to ratify or accede to the FA-PT before it enters into force. We look forward to see which five countries will take up the role of championing the region in this important area.

---

[3] For details, see draft implementation road map at: http://www.unescap.org/resources/road-map-implementation-substantive-provisions-framework-agreement-facilitation-cross

References

ADB and ESCAP (2017). "Trade Facilitation and Better Connectivity for an Inclusive Asia and Pacific", ADB. Available at: https://www.adb.org/publications/trade-facilitation-connectivity-inclusive-asia-pacific

Duval, Y., and Kong, M. (2017). "Digital Trade Facilitation: Paperless Trade in Regional Trade Agreements", *ADBI Working Paper Series*, ADBI. Available at: https://www.adb.org/sites/default/files/publication/321851/adbi-wp747.pdf

Shepherd, B., and Duval, Y. (2015). "Estimating the Benefits of Cross-Border Paperless Trade", in Reducing Trade Costs in Asia and the Pacific, Studies in Trade and Investment No. 84, *ESCAP*, United Nations. Available at: http://www.unescap.org/publications/reducing-trade-costs-asia-pacific-developing-countries-studies-trade-and-investment-no

United Nations (2016). *Framework Agreement on Facilitation of Cross-border Paperless Trade in Asia and the Pacific.* Available at: http://www.un.org/ga/search/view_doc.asp?symbol=E/ESCAP/RES/72/4&Lang=E

Xue, H. (2017). The Newest UN Treaty to Facilitate Cross-Border Paperless Trade in Asia and the Pacific: An Insight Preview. Journal of World Trade Volume 51, Issue 6, pp. 959-985. Available at http://www.kluwerlawonline.com/abstract.php?area-Journals&id=TRAD2017038

Conclusion and way forward

This study presented the state of play in trade facilitation implementation in Asia and the Pacific. It confirmed the importance of moving from paper-based to digital trade processes to reduce trade costs, which remain too high for many countries and stakeholders in the region to effectively participate and benefit from import and export activities. The need for paperless trading has been acknowledged in many bilateral and regional trade agreements since the mid-1990s, but actual implementation has been slow and often limited to pilot projects and/or bilateral exchanges of specific documents. Arguably the most advanced plurilateral cross-border paperless trade initiative of the region, the ASEAN Single Window (ASW) has seen significant delays since it was launched in 2005 and its implementation remained partial as of 2017, essentially limited to exchange of the preferential certificate of origin (CEPT Form D) among a subset of ASEAN members on a pilot basis. It provides, however, a useful basis for some of the digital trade facilitation solutions to be developed under the Framework Agreement on Facilitation of Cross-border Paperless Trade in Asia and the Pacific (FA-PT).

New technologies and innovative services have emerged which greatly facilitate procedures between private sector actors (businesses or individual consumers), potentially making trade much more inclusive and sustainable. The emergence of e-commerce platforms and services in particular has made commercial procedures much easier than before. Transport and payment procedures have also become easier as trade-support services are increasingly integrated into these platforms, which are often accessible from anywhere in the world. However, much of the cross-border e-commerce potential remains untapped. Trade regulations themselves aside, this may be attributed in part to the fact that regulatory procedures are not aligned with these new ways of doing business. Enabling trade control agencies to take advantage of the fact that the original data generated and used by private sector stakeholders are now almost always in electronic form would go a long way in facilitating trade – and increasing regulatory compliance. Development of mobile applications for completion of regulatory procedures may also be actively considered as, unlike computers, these devices have become ubiquitous in even the least developed countries of the region. Finally, establishing public-private partnerships between trade control agencies and the e-commerce, e-payment and/or e-logistics platforms may be explored to transfer part of the regulatory control functions to these private service sector providers, taking advantage of their IT capabilities and know-how, as well as their privileged access to data.

As pairs or larger groups of countries in the region continue to develop facilities to exchange electronic data and documents for trade facilitation and regulatory compliance, it is crucial that they share information and lessons learned with each other to ensure the systems being developed are interoperable at both the legal and technical levels. While it is rational that countries focus on the development of intra-national systems first (national or port single windows), these systems – including related laws and regulations – should be designed with cross-border exchange of electronic data and documents in mind. In fact, as the cost of developing a cross-border enabled system is not expected to be significantly higher than that of a paperless trade system designed for intra-national exchange of data and documents, less developed countries with no legacy systems may take the opportunity to leapfrog from manual systems to world-leading paperless systems.

Looking ahead, standards and solutions for digital trade facilitation will continue to evolve rapidly. Innovations such as blockchain and distributed ledger technology (DLT),[1] as well as progress in machine learning and artificial intelligence (AI), and the development of the internet of things (IoT) have enormous potential in making international supply chains more transparent and efficient. DLT could remove the need for documents altogether, with everyone involved in a trade transaction relying on data recorded in shared ledgers and managed through smart contracts, also providing new opportunities for supply chain financing and traceability. AI systems trained using accumulated data on transactions and decisions found in customs and other trade control agencies existing systems could take risk management to the next level, further reducing the need for physical inspections of large number of products. IoT could enable vehicles, containers, storage facilities, scanners to communicate directly among themselves about their

---

[1]   See, for example, https://www.gov.uk/government/uploads/system/uploads/attachment_data/file/492972/gs-16-1-distributed-ledger-technology.pdf

location, availability, need for maintenance, etc. making their use more efficient and reducing needs for additional equipment and physical infrastructure. However, meaningful implementation of these technologies for trade facilitation will require much coordination and cooperation among stakeholders.

As highlighted and promoted in the FA-PT, implementation of digital trade facilitation should be undertaken based on existing international standards whenever possible. An important starting point here is the adoption by both public and private stakeholders of data models based on those developed under the auspices of the United Nations and the World Customs Organization. On the legal side, adoption of key principles embedded in UNCITRAL instruments such as the United Nations Convention on the Use of Electronic Communications in International Contracts (ECC) would be important in advancing cross-border paperless trade.[2] The new UNCITRAL Model Law on Electronic Transferable Records adopted in July 2017 also provides a potentially very useful new standard and way forward for enabling cross-border legal recognition of key commercial documents such as electronic bills of lading.[3]

Pending entry into force of the FA-PT, the Interim Intergovernmental Steering Group on Cross-border Paperless Trade Facilitation (IISG-CPTF) and the United Nations Network of Experts for Paperless Trade and Transport in Asia and the Pacific (UNNExT), both under the auspices of ESCAP, offer dedicated and inclusive regional platforms for building capacity and enhancing collaboration on digital trade facilitation. Legal and technical-readiness assessment tools and lists of available international standards and conventions that can facilitate safe and secure electronic exchange of trade data and documents have already been developed through these two platforms, and studies are being conducted on how to achieve mutual recognition of electronic data and documents.

Going forward, it will be important for development partners to ramp up capacity building and technical assistance to digital trade facilitation. Such support may be provided under existing facilities, including those linked to the Aid for Trade initiative or the implementation of the WTO Trade Facilitation Agreement. Assistance should cover both technical and legal aspects and include support for ICT infrastructure development as well as for addressing cybersecurity threats, two foundational elements for a successful journey towards safe, secure and seamless cross-border paperless trade. Meantime, developing countries themselves should strive to enhance and further institutionalize inter-agency and public-private sector collaboration in this area, possibly by integrating paperless trade into the work of their existing National Trade Facilitation Committees (NTFC).[4]

---

[2] These are in fact specifically reflected in the General Principles of the FA-PT (Art. 5).

[3] The increased legal certainty provided for in the model law potentially removes a major obstacle to the use by trade control agencies of the original data generated and used by private sector stakeholders. See http://www.uncitral.org/uncitral/en/uncitral_texts/electronic_commerce/2017model.html

[4] Establishment of an NTFC is required under the WTO TFA.